Cambridge Elements ≡

Elements in Religion and Violence
edited by
James R. Lewis
University of Tromsø
Margo Kitts
Hawai'i Pacific University

THE PROBLEM OF JOB AND THE PROBLEM OF EVIL

Espen Dahl
UiT The Arctic University of Norway

CAMBRIDGE
UNIVERSITY PRESS

CAMBRIDGE
UNIVERSITY PRESS

University Printing House, Cambridge CB2 8BS, United Kingdom

One Liberty Plaza, 20th Floor, New York, NY 10006, USA

477 Williamstown Road, Port Melbourne, VIC 3207, Australia

314–321, 3rd Floor, Plot 3, Splendor Forum, Jasola District Centre,
New Delhi – 110025, India

79 Anson Road, #06–04/06, Singapore 079906

Cambridge University Press is part of the University of Cambridge.

It furthers the University's mission by disseminating knowledge in the pursuit of
education, learning, and research at the highest international levels of excellence.

www.cambridge.org
Information on this title: www.cambridge.org/9781108723299
DOI: 10.1017/9781108613743

First published 2019

A catalogue record for this publication is available from the British Library.

ISBN 978-1-108-72329-9 Paperback
ISSN 2397-9496 (online)
ISSN 2514-3786 (print)

Cambridge Elements

The Problem of Job and the Problem of Evil

DOI: 10.1017/9781108613743
First published online: December 2018

Espen Dahl
UiT The Arctic University of Norway

ABSTRACT: This account of evil takes the Book of Job as its guide. The Book of Job considers physical pain, social bereavement, the origin of evil, theodicy, justice, divine violence, and reward. Such problems are explored by consulting ancient and modern accounts from the fields of theology and philosophy, broadly conceived. Some of the literature on evil – especially the philosophical literature – is inclined toward the abstract treatment of such problems. Bringing along the suffering Job serves as a reminder of the concrete, lived experience in which the problem of evil has its roots.

KEYWORDS: evil, Job, theodicy, pain

ISBNs: 9781108723299 (PB), 9781108613743 (OC)
ISSNs: 2397-9496 (online), 2514-3786 (print)

Contents

Introduction

"There was once a man in the land of Uz whose name was Job. That man was blameless and upright, one who feared God and turned away from evil" (Job 1:1).[1] Thus starts one of the most renowned accounts of innocent suffering in world literature. It starts well – almost too well; like a fairy tale or a fable, it places the hero in an unidentifiable past in a place far away. Job has a large family and significant wealth, and he makes sure that he observes God's commands. How could anything possibly go wrong? The Book of Job invites us to imagine this atmosphere of fulfillment and happiness. Its attraction is perhaps not only its depiction of a wishful state, but also its portrayal of a situation in which everything makes sense: there is correspondence between virtue and health, work and proliferation, sacrifice and God's benevolence. There is nothing troubling on the horizon, no reason to ask questions; everything adds up to the harmonious unity of life before God. But, as we know, the situation soon changes. Satan enters the story and all kinds of evil befall this righteous man.

It has been noted that pleasure is heedless of the metaphysical – it directs us merely toward the continuation of life as it is and its acceptance without question. Well-being is a state in which we can remain unreflective about ourselves and our surroundings. Suffering, however, calls for attention and thought. In disturbing our expectations and desires, breaking into our lives and bereaving us of what we care for, suffering gives rise to thought. In suffering, some kind of evil irrupts our lives, and things can no longer be taken as matters of course (Buytendijk 1961: 24–26). Evil has many faces: pain, death, violence,

---

[1] All references to and quotations from the Book of Job are taken from the New Revised Standard Version of the Bible.

rape, depression, starvation, perpetration, war, earthquakes, tsunamis – the list is endless. In all these cases, life, the world, and – for believers such as Job – God no longer make up a seamless unity. Bodies break down and cease to respond in the way that we expect them to; souls are darkened, unable to appreciate what they found in life before. Dignity turns to shame, and losses break down vital relations and throw us back upon ourselves. These are different modes through which the destructive force we call "evil" ruins what is worthwhile in life. For the suffering Job too, reality becomes different – it is no longer to be taken for granted and is rendered highly questionable, to say the least. The first expression of this questionable state is "Why?": "Why me? Why this way? Why now?" There may well be natural explanations for disease, social and psychological dysfunction, and biological and geological events. While, doubtless, scientific explanations are of much use, they hardly ever answer the "Why?" questions of the sufferer. Such a "Why?" is posed in another register – the spiritual, the existential, the emotional, or perhaps all of these at the same time.

The role of religion in suffering is ambivalent. It can certainly comfort if there is, say, a touch of love despite everything or some hidden, deeper purpose, or perhaps a final restoration in this life or after. But religion might also be felt to be deflecting the real problem, as Job obviously comes to regard his friends' "comfort"; they refuse to see the injustice of the suffering and, perhaps most importantly, they fail to attend to Job's suffering. For Job, the evil of suffering is doubtless; God, however, raises doubt. This is one way to formulate what in modern times has become known as the problem of evil. Put in the simplest form: how could the good and almighty God allow evil to happen? It cannot be denied that the problem of evil is an acute one, especially when it is not regarded as an intellectual puzzle but is drawing near in life. Evil has certainly made people lose faith, but it has also led people to faith – to find a deeper resonance or perhaps a meaning for why evil happens. It is probable that, in most cases, the onset of evil changes faith, as I believe it does eventually for Job (Larrimore 2001: xiv). In this case, the unproblematic acceptance of traditional outlooks must go through the trial of evil, and faith can be returned to only through the redefinition of the traditions that were left. Naïvety is lost on the way and a new form of acknowledgment is called for, tempered by the experiences of evil, non-sense, and pain. However one reads the contested later chapters of Job, from the God in the whirlwind to Job's final restoration, it is indisputable that Job's faith changes significantly.

By addressing some of the central components of the drama of Job, I have indicated the theme of this Element. It concerns the problem of evil – or, more specifically, of suffering evil – and the ways it is reflected on within religious frameworks. A swift search on the Internet will confirm that there is no end of literature in this field, both historically speaking and in contemporary debates. Despite the secular age that has emerged in the West, the discussions have not ceased. This is due, I assume, not only to some sort of "return" of religion in politics and academia but also to the fact that encountering evil calls for thought – thought that, sooner or later, for better or worse, touches religious dimensions (and, at times, denial thereof). A small book like this cannot cover the vast body of available literature and hence requires some confining principles. Having taken the Book of Job as my point of departure, I continue to employ it as my guide throughout this volume. The intention is not to dive into a close reading of the text but, rather, to dwell on some of the central problems that it raises. These problems are explored by consulting ancient and modern accounts from the fields of theology and philosophy, broadly conceived.

Being a classical text, the Book of Job has earned its status by being read and interpreted over and over again for about 2,500 years, and it certainly has a massive reception history: Jewish, Christian, and, to some extent, Muslim. As part of culture, it continues to work silently, forging ways to question and respond to the problem of evil. The text considers physical pain, social bereavement, the origin of evil, theodicy, justice, divine violence, and reward – problems to which I return in due course. Some of the literature on evil – especially the philosophical literature – is inclined toward the abstract treatment of current problems, turning them rather sterile and pale in the face of actual suffering. While there are legitimate reasons for keeping a distance from real evil and suffering when thinking critically, there is a point at which the distance becomes so big that the source from which it arose is lost from sight. Hopefully, bringing along the suffering Job will keep reminding us, in the way that perhaps only literature can remind us, of the lived experience in which the problem of evil has its original home.

What Is the Problem of Evil?

Job's story approaches the question of evil from a particular perspective: that of the innocent sufferer. In this Element, pain, suffering, and evil are regarded as closely related. While there are internal connections between the three, they are not completely identical. Pain emphasizes the physical dimension, while suffering is a wider category that includes psychological, existential, and religious dimensions. Evil occurs where pain or suffering come with a certain intensity and a lack of obvious reason, desert, or motivation. But there are forms of pain and suffering that are not obviously evil, such as pain as a signal of danger or the pain of growth (both physical and social). There is also evil that does not correspond directly with suffering, such as damage to valuable things, natural catastrophes, and the like. Yet it seems that there must still be someone, if not directly, at least indirectly suffering as a result of such destruction in order for it to be called "evil" because evil relates, directly or indirectly, to sentient beings vulnerable to suffering. Hence, suffering is the primary place in which the phenomenon of evil becomes manifest (Dalferth 2006a: 29).

Given this rough delineation of the central notions within this text, it is possible to look at the setup of the problem of evil in some more detail. Most of the philosophical problems and interpretations of suffering and evil that are dealt with in this volume presuppose a monotheistic backdrop. Still, it is true that the problem was known about and considered within Greek philosophy, prior to any known exchange of ideas with the Hebrew monotheistic tradition. Of course, the Greek treatment of suffering and evil is marked by another cultural setting and preferences for other conceptions, indeed, against another religious horizon than that which we find in the Hebrew Bible. Nevertheless, the convergences are significant, and therefore the Greek accounts can be regarded as an interesting anticipation of the way in which two different traditions – Athens and Jerusalem – grew into one another during the Hellenistic and later Roman periods, having an enormous impact on spirituality and thought in the West and beyond. Tellingly, the most famous formulation of the problem of evil, written by Epicurus, is known to us thanks to a quotation by a Christian theologian, Lactantius, in the fourth century. It reads:

> God either wishes to take away evils and he cannot, or he neither wishes to nor is able, or he both wishes and is able. If he wishes to and is not able, he is feeble, which does not fall in with the notion of god. If he is able to and does not wish to, he is envious, which is equally foreign to god. If he neither wishes to nor is able, he is both envious and feeble and therefore not god. If he both wishes to and is able, which alone is fitting to god, whence, therefore, are there evils, and why does he not remove them? (Lactantius 2001: 50)

Although, admittedly, having the Greek gods in mind, Epicurus's argument presupposes a conception of God that is shared by the monotheistic traditions as well. It turns on the perfection that is bound up with the analytical concept of God: God must be perfectly almighty and also perfectly good, yet evil undeniably exists. One does not need to be a logician to see that this trilemma does not add up (Mackie 1971: 92).

There are many ways in which to respond to the problem of evil. If there is a pantheon of gods, as in polytheism, one can distribute good and evil to different gods, just as with other qualities, and thus the problem evaporates. Or one can assume a cosmic dualism, where two forces are in a permanent state of war. But if one is discussing the problem of evil within the framework of monotheism, these options are precluded from the beginning. Hence, what seems like the most logical answer to the problem is to eliminate God. Such a solution, sometimes called "the argument from evil," turns the fact of evil into an argument against the existence of God (Inwagen 2008: 4). It is not only logically valid but there is also robust evidence on its side: we can experience evil empirically, but empirical evidence for God is hard to provide – if we are claiming universal consent, at least. Remarkably, for all his suffering, protests, and even sacrilegious sayings, for Job, God's existence is beyond dispute; it is within this faith the problem unfolds. In the West, the refusal of God did not become a viable option until modern times. Before that, God was, so to speak, built into the framework of the worldview (Taylor 2007: 3).

The tradition of modern theodicy, made famous by Leibniz's work with the same name from 1710, aims at justifying God in the face of what seem to be compelling accusations. Compared with biblical accounts, there is more than a hint of a new understanding of God and the world in Leibniz's endeavor. Whereas Job wants to have his case tested before a divine court in order to learn the reason for his suffering, the tables have turned in modern theodicy: God is charged and it is up to the apologetic philosopher to defend him with rational arguments. Whatever implications such a reversal has, it makes clear, at least, that God can no longer be accepted simply as an integral part of a commonly shared worldview. Along with secularization, a new conception of suffering has also emerged. Even if suffering has always led to outcries and complaints, it used to be regarded as a necessary part of life, as testified by the laments of the Psalms. During the Middle Ages, mystics even regarded pain as a privileged gateway permitting an experience of God. At some point during modernity, not least due to new medical competence, suffering came to be regarded as an exception essentially foreign to life. In this light, modern theodicy becomes doubly acute: both God and suffering have lost their roles as immediately meaningful givens (Larrimore 2001: xxix).

There is no doubt that eliminating God solves the logical problem of the trilemma mentioned earlier in this Element. However, for those who have suffered evil, there might also be other, existential reasons for rejecting God: not because of a lack of argument or conviction but due to rage and hate, acts of rejection that, paradoxically, confirm the very existence of God. Such a position might lead to protests against God, which have been widespread in the Jewish tradition since the time of Job. But it might also lead to atheism. However, atheism might not offer as easy a "solution" to the existential problem of evil as it seems because even after the elimination of God, the sting of evil does not disappear. The "Why?" of suffering does not vanish with God but is, it appears, built into the experience of pain, suffering, and injustice (Dahl 2017). Even a confirmed atheist expects goodness in life – otherwise, evil would not be offensive (Moltmann 1981: 48; Løgstrup 1995: 225). But then, the problem strangely recurs in a new form: from whence can this goodness come?

There are, however, other routes out of the trilemma of the omnipotence of God, the goodness of God, and the evil in the world (Meister 2012: 6–10). One might seek to qualify the notion of God's omnipotence either by admitting that there are forces within His creation that restrain His power or by delegating responsibility for evil to free human beings. Alternatively, one may qualify the absolute goodness of God by claiming that there is also a hidden and potentially frightening side to God. And the list goes on. In the subsequent sections, I give attention to the most important of these responses to the problem of evil, creating an interplay between these and the problem of Job.

The Reception of Job

Although the problem of evil has echoes in many religions, the logical exigency of the matter is most pressing, arguably, in monotheistic religions due to the obvious tension between evil and the notion of one good and all-powerful God (Cenkner 1997). In choosing Job as my guide, I have also conceded that the religious scope of this investigation is limited to the monotheistic tradition. Versions of the story originally circulated in various oral and, later, written forms, and most scholars think that the prologue and epilogue of the Book of Job are composed from such preexisting folktales. Included in the Hebrew Bible, Tanakh, the Book of Job later became part of what Christians came to call the Old Testament of the Bible and was preserved, therefore, in both traditions. The figure of Job also found his way into the Qur'an – only in four brief passages, but, nevertheless, not without making some impact. Perhaps it is the lack of a clear identity that makes Job such a widely accessible figure: the events happened once upon a time and in a distant place: Uz. Even though legends and early commentaries suggest that Job was an Egyptian, a Jew, or perhaps a Gentile prophet, his identity has remained essentially open.

No interpretation of a text can reach a detached "God's point of view" from which its ultimate meaning is reached. In fact, a text can make sense only within the possibilities and limitations of a specific cultural tradition. This holds true especially for a classical text – a text handed down over a long period of time and continually reread and reinterpreted, according to shifting times and contexts. Being one such classical text, the Book of Job has been approached at various temporal junctures and has been situated in different religious and cultural contexts. Looking more closely at the nature of the text, it has proved hard to settle on a date for its composition. Most likely, it found its final form sometime between the sixth century and the fourth century BC. It might very well have been worked over in various phases. One indication that this is the case is that the prologue (Job 1–2) and epilogue (Job 42:7–17) are written in prose and offer a different portrayal of Job from that given in the dialogues, which are written in poetic language. There was probably a separate folktale about Job, which we meet in an elaborated version in the prologue and epilogue; the poetic part may have been of later origin and grafted onto the folktale. Moreover, there is also a long speech by Elihu in chapters 32–37 that suddenly enters the dialogue between Job and his three friends. Elihu is not presented at the outset of the story and enters at a point where the dialogue seems to have reached its end. For such reasons, scholars have argued that the text contains several later interpolations.

If we focus on the version that became part of the Bible, it has a relatively clear structure:

- *Prologue*: 1–2. The narrative takes place in Heaven and on Earth. Job is tested twice.
- *Dialogues*: 3–38. The three friends Elifas, Bildad, and Sofar are defending God, arguing that suffering is a punishment for some form of transgression. Job declares his innocence. Finally, a fourth person, Elihu, delivers the last speech against Job.
- *God's speech*: 39–42:6. God finally speaks to Job and exhibits His power as Creator, His inscrutable depths, and the beauty and horror of His creation.
- *Epilogue*: 42:7–16. The text returns to the folktale genre. Job is finally deemed righteous by God and his property and family are restored.

In the early Jewish commentaries Talmud and Midrash, Job's origin is hotly discussed, being a question that is obviously important to Jewish identity.

Even though there is a current that holds that Job was innocent, the major tendency among ancient Jewish commentators is to argue that Job deserved what happened to him, either due to his life prior to the story that is recorded or because Job is guilty of arrogating God's position in the dialogue. Talmudic commentaries also tend to play down the harshest protests of Job and to stress that God changes his fortunes in the end (Glatzer 1969: 17–18). During the Middle Ages, the focus shifted toward the problem of reconciling the Job of the prologue with the Job of the dialogue – the pious Job and the rebellious Job. There are mystical and speculative accounts, such as *Zoha* by Moses de Leon, but the most influential account was put forward by Moses Maimonides in the thirteenth century. Although Job is only allotted two chapters in Maimonides's *The Guide for the Perplexed*, Maimonides's reading, combining Judaic thought and Aristotelian philosophy, has been very influential. Job is regarded as virtuous when it comes to conduct; yet, according to Maimonides, he lacks proper wisdom. The wisdom Job learns gradually through suffering is that true happiness is not tied to earthly possessions, health, and children, but to true knowledge of God (Maimonides 2000: 74).

In early Christian commentaries, Job is mentioned almost exclusively in references to the folktale of the prologue and epilogue (Nemo 1998: 12–13). And understandably so, because this avoids the troublesome issue of the rebellious Job being on the brink of blasphemy. In the line of interpreters, from Tertullian through Ambrose to Augustine, Job is almost invariably taken as an example of patience that subjects himself obediently to God (Seow 2013: 181–187). The most influential commentary on Job is, however, Gregor the Great's *Magna Moralia*, completed around 590. This work not only influenced the depiction of Job throughout the Middle Ages but was also important for the establishment of the biblical exegesis that ensued. Gregor's program was to gloss the entire Book of Job with exegesis showing how the text refers simultaneously to three levels of meaning: the historical or literal meaning, the allegorical or spiritual meaning, and the moral meaning. Through this threefold interpretation, he suggested that all the basic Christian doctrines were reflected in the Book of Job, including Christ, the Trinity, the Holy Church, and so on (Seow 2013: 194).

Job, or Johab, has also played a role in Islam, even if not as significant as in Judaism and Christianity. From the four short passages in the Qur'an, a picture of Johab emerges. According to the Qur'an, Johab is a prophet whose primary characteristic is outstanding patience. His faith withstands the trouble that he goes through; he suffers without knowing why, yet he clings to his reliable God and is rewarded in return (Burrell 2008: 78–80). In short, this account of Job repeats the central features of the folktale, with some variations and additions, and is in line with early Judaic and Christian interpretations: Job is an example to follow. In *Stories of the Prophet*, compiled in the ninth century, a richer reservoir of stories emerges. Interestingly, Job's wife, Rahma, is given a much more positive depiction – indeed, she is portrayed as God's vehicle for divine grace (Seow 2013: 245). While there are various opinions on Job's lot in Christian and early Judaic interpretations, Islam is consistent in stressing that Job's suffering is undeserved. However, as Navid Kermani argues, while the more troublesome aspects of Job are more or less constantly repressed in the Christian inheritance of the book, Islam gradually comes to acknowledge his quarreling with God; in fact, that quarrel even develops into a topos of its own in Muslim mystical literature (Kermani 2011: 129–131).

Moving on to modern times, starting with the Reformation, we find a new sensitivity toward language, philology, and interpretation that paves the way for another reception of the Book of Job. However, even in Luther, for whom the hidden and dark sides of God are acknowledged, we can find something reserved about the account of the Book of Job. For Luther, the book's question is whether or not misfortune can come to the righteous from God – and, indeed, Job shows that it can. Therefore, the friends are wrong when they regard it as punishment – particularly because this opinion lowers the conception of God to worldly standards. While Luther does not downplay the dialogues, he still holds that Job speaks wrongly about God when he protests (Luther 2001: 135). Like Luther, Calvin does not want to acknowledge Job's protest. In his view, the moral of the Book of Job is that we must learn to keep our mouths shut (Glatzer 1969: 33–34).

The hierarchy implied in the distinction between God and man was challenged in many ways during the Enlightenment period. The growing trust in human reason meant that any acceptance of earthly and heavenly knowledge had to pass the tribunal of human reason. Kant was, on one hand, quintessentially modern, insofar as he thought that no traditional doctrine or tradition should be accepted without an appeal to reason. On the other hand, however, he regarded reason as having its own conditions and limits. For Kant, not only do arguments regarding the existence of God fall outside the logic of reason, so too does theodicy. According to Kant, Job's friends are wrong because they insist on both unfailing earthly and divine justice. Job is right, therefore, to reject their theodicy and to maintain his own notion of God, even though it is irreconcilable with his experience. God lets him see the inscrutable depths of His creation, including the destructive parts that do not fit into human conceptions of purpose and reason. Kant (2001: 232) concludes that it is beyond our competence to judge God.

The Second World War is another watershed in the reception of Job – especially the Jewish reception. The question is no longer about possible sins on Job's part or about the pious and patient Job; rather, Job becomes a figure of identification for the Jewish people post-Holocaust. Martin Buber places stress on the dialogical relationship between people and God. He contends that the text spoke originally of Job as a stand-in for the people of Israel and that, correspondingly, we can speak of the "Job of the gas chambers" in modern times (Buber 1967: 224). Elie Wiesel, who himself survived Auschwitz, also links Job with the destiny of the Jewish people, seeing him as a contemporary. While Job certainly suffers, it is not the patient Job but the protesting version who stands in the foreground of Wiesel's reading. Straight after the war, Wiesel (1976: 233–234) suggests, this suffering figure could "be seen on every road of Europe. Wounded, robbed, mutilated. Certainly not happy. Nor resigned." Job turns his speech directly toward God, crossing taboos and profanation, and argues against God's abuse. While the dominant interpretation of Job in modern Islam focuses on the exemplary virtues of Job, we can also find voices that follow in the footsteps of Wiesel's Job: the Job who revolts against the terror of God (Kermani 2011).

As this brief sketch has tried to make clear, there is no one way to read Job, and there is no one solution to the problem of evil. For most of the history of the reception of the Book of Job, these two elements have been discussed together: reading Job offers a way to grapple with present experiences of evil. It must be remembered, however, that the present also informs the reading, influencing what aspects stand out as particularly significant. The following sections examine the main parts of the Book of Job, each beginning with a short presentation of the part from the Book of Job under discussion, before elaborating on the significant contributions of these parts in relation to the problem of evil.

1 The Prologue: The Nature of Evil

As already noted, the story of Job begins with a state of almost perfect happiness. Job, we learn, is morally blameless and upstanding. He is a pious man who fears God, and he is blessed by God in return: God makes him into one of the wealthiest men in the East. As the scene changes and we find ourselves watching a gathering of heavenly beings before God in Heaven, we note that Satan is among those beings. The plot takes off as Satan asks: "Does Job fear God for nothing?" (Job 1:9), after which God grants Satan permission to test Job.

Where does evil come from? And what is its nature? In the Book of Job, it enters in the figure of Satan (*hassatan* – literally, "the accuser" or "the adversary") and by the suffering he inflicts: first by destroying Job's house, livelihood, servants, and children, and later by striking Job down with a painful disease. Having been afflicted with loss and suffering twice over, Job eventually falls silent for seven days and seven nights (Job 2:13). Even though there are other evils in the world that are not directly addressed – such as natural catastrophes, social repression, and murder – the story still has sufficiently wide ramifications to serve as a fruitful starting point for the discussion of the nature of evil. Before exploring some central aspects of the nature of evil, it is worth investigating what this strange figure of Satan can possibly signify.

Satan and the Serpent

It is striking that in the Book of Job, Satan does not have the power that he seems to have in the New Testament, where he can tempt Jesus, cause obsession in people, and even take the shape of a big dragon entangled in a cosmic battle (the latter perhaps drawing on Leviathan as depicted in God's speech to Job in Job 41). Satan is mentioned in passing in two other places in the Hebrew Bible (1 Chron. 12:1; Zech. 3:1–3), each time as a minor figure tempting or accusing others. The two initial chapters of the Book of Job are, in fact, the most sustained accounts of Satan in the entire Old Testament, an account that fits into the picture drawn in the other passages: he is not a demonic, powerful antipode to God, but one of His divine beings – one that raises problems and conflicts. Satan does so not as a fully free and autonomous agent, but only within the limitations set by God (Wray and Mobley 2005: 63).

In approaching God, Satan is not making claims or judgments; instead, just like the serpent in the Garden of Eden, he raises questions and thereby insinuates things indirectly and shrewdly. When the Lord brags about the outstanding righteousness of Job, Satan replies with a question: "Have you not put a fence around him and his house and all that he has, on every side?" (Job 1:10), suggesting that, far from being motivated by gratuitous devotion, Job has found that piety has simply proved profitable. Thus, it is by playing Devil's advocate that Satan sows the seed of doubt, and once such doubt has been sown, it is hard to repress – even God gives in to it (Newsom 2009: 56). And so Job is subjected to a horrible ordeal, the aim of which is not to test Job's tolerance for suffering but his reason for holding on to God.

Of course, Satan is far from innocent in this story, which becomes evident from the suffering he inflicts on Job. Even if some biblical scholars argue that to equate Job's Satan with the principle of evil is to impose elements of meaning that are lacking in the original text, this mythical figure nevertheless has some telling traits that are worthwhile exploring in relation to evil. For a monotheistic religion, there can be no question of a symmetrical dualism between good and evil, God and Satan. Since God is the Creator of good creation, it remains very hard to fit evil into that picture. Of course, in some stories, God Himself seems cruel – to many modern readers, the Book of Job is certainly among them. But if one traces the development of the religion presented in the Hebrew Bible, the violent and capricious side of God tends to be purged of ambiguity.

However good God and creation might eventually be, forces remain that work against the good within creation. Of course, the Devil, demons, evil spirits, and Satan can be regarded as mythical images of this evilness that remains, even if they do not fit into a strictly monotheistic scheme. Hence, we are left with an ambiguous situation, in which evil must be acknowledged as present in the created world, but still does not belong properly to it. In the prologue of the Book of Job, Satan's ambiguous nature is emphasized. He is among those who gather in heaven before God, yet he seems to be a stranger there, as flagged by God's question: "Where have you come from?" Satan's answer confirms his lack of belonging not only in Heaven but also on Earth: "From going to and fro on the Earth, and from walking up and down on it" (Job 1:8; cf. Stump 2012: 197–199). This is, however, more than an evasive gesture; it indicates something important about the nature of Satan: his lack of a proper place in creation. Not only has he been everywhere and nowhere on Earth but, since the conversation is set in Heaven, Satan must also travel between Earth and Heaven – and, it must be assumed, is not at home in either. Although a heavenly being, he does not dwell in Heaven, and he is not, properly speaking, an earthly creature. If we read this as a myth that reveals something about the nature of evil, then it seems to say that evil does not fit in anywhere but is still potentially everywhere. Evil neither stems from God nor is part of the creation that was made "very good" (Gen. 1:31). A similar point can be made without any religious connotations: undergoing evil, when in pain or when suffering otherwise, one encounters something that should not exist; since it exists, however, it disrupts the categories and expectations that orient our lives in the world (Bernstein 2015: 12, 94).

The figure most commonly associated with Satan is the serpent in Genesis. Plenty of monsters populated the religious imagination in the Near East of the time, from which the biblical scriptures have borrowed a significant amount. Indeed, Leviathan and Behemoth in the Book of Job and the serpent in Genesis share some of these monsters' traits. Curiously, Genesis does not mention evil monsters, Satan, or the Devil. There is simply a serpent, which, we learn, is regarded as the most cunning of God's creatures (Gen. 3:1). The association between the serpent and Satan is a later interpretation, probably stemming from the New Testament (Rev. 12:9) and elaborated at length in the Christian West since Augustine. As the story of Eden is meant, no doubt, to give an account of the troublesome nature of the human condition, and as the serpent is a significant figure in the story, it makes sense to interrogate that myth too, where evil is concerned. The question to ask here, then, is: how did evil enter the human world?

The cunning serpent says: "Did God say, 'You shall not eat from any tree in the garden?'" (Gen. 3:1), a question that more than suggests that God has arbitrarily held something back from Adam and Eve. The parallel with Job's Satan is striking: the serpent begins with something as innocent as a question. Moreover, the serpent also symbolizes the ambivalent structure delineated earlier. The preceding story of the creation in seven days depicts the gradual emergence of a well-ordered universe, with water below, Earth in the middle, and the sky above, and in which all creatures are assigned a place. The serpent, however, can climb trees, swim in the water, and crawl on Earth and hence move across the distinct spheres; it does not seem to find its proper place in any one of them. Mary Douglas (2002: 44, 69–70), discussing understandings of impurity in the Hebrew Bible, claims that the impure (and, hence, potentially dangerous) is what falls outside systems and neat categories. In this sense, the serpent is impure: "matter out of place." This point suggests that evil cannot be positioned fully within the order of being – and particularly not within the good creation. It is an impure category that disrupts the constitutive order of the world.

In the story of Eden, the serpent is not just part of Adam and Eve's story; its function is, in fact, to instigate the fatal transgression, the consequences of which are still part of our existence today. Paul Ricoeur has given the serpent an interpretation that reflects the human condition as we know it: first, it signifies some kind of externality of temptation, meaning that evil somehow comes from outside oneself and is something to which one, more or less passively, yields. In this respect, the serpent might be taken as a projection of inner temptations, as Ricoeur contends. Second, notably, the serpent is "always already there," in the temporal sense, as if evil is already lying in wait as one becomes its agent. Third, each individual comes into a world in which s/he is not the inventor of evil, but in which evil is transmitted by human traditions and then picked up later by individuals. In sum, the serpent is the symbol of a strange prior state of evil. To give in to evil or to fall is less than destiny and more than choice. With regard to human enactment, Ricoeur (1967: 259) writes: "the always-already-there of evil is the *other* aspect of the evil for which, nevertheless, *I* am responsible."

What Is Evil?

Even if it is difficult to define evil due to its ambiguous and evasive nature, it has become common to distinguish between three different types of evil, a division famously first made by Leibniz (2017: 92). First, there is moral evil, which entails personal responsibility: one actively does something harmful, while another suffers the consequences thereof. In religious language, this is sin. Second, there is physical or natural evil, in the shape of earthquakes, tsunamis, disabilities, and illness – that is, states or events that cause suffering, without any morally responsible agent to blame. Finally, there is metaphysical evil, which has to do with the very condition of life and the world in general: essentially, their imperfection, in the sense of being subject to change and limitations. It is from this metaphysical perspective that one can discuss why our world contains evil and suffering in the first place.

For all its clarity, this tripartite structure does not allow evil to be categorized as easily as is suggested. There are cases in which it is difficult to categorize evil as either moral or physical – for instance, natural disasters that stem from human-made climate change. And there is collective human action, such as participation in the Holocaust, that can neither be reduced to individual moral choices nor be seen simply as an event (Dalferth 2006a: 12–17). If we keep in mind the problem of evil as presented in Job, it too cuts across such distinctions. Obviously, there is natural evil in the form of suffering and pain, but it is depicted as if someone – God or Satan – stands behind it. Moreover, Job's illness and the loss of his property and children also seem to be placed in between moral and natural evil: the roof falls down during a storm, but killing and looting also occur. As soon as God replies to Job from the whirlwind (Job 38–40), we are offered a metaphysical perspective in response to moral and natural evils. What these examples remind us of is that, as useful as the distinction between moral, natural, and metaphysical evil may be, it offers no more than a set of heuristic categories that provides some initial orientation into the messy world of evil.

Historically speaking, it is safe to say that Augustine ranks among those who has had the most decisive impact on Western thought on evil – partly on sin and moral evil (to which I return in the next section), and partly on metaphysical evil, on which I focus here. Committed to monotheistic logic and informed by Neoplatonic metaphysics, Augustine sees the problem as how to preserve the notion of a perfectly good and changeless God in the face of evil, without opening up any kind of dualism – say, an autonomous evil principle, substance, or force. Evil cannot derive from the good Creator, and yet it is there; it is not a thing, but not nothing, either.

Augustine views all reality as hierarchically ordered. God ranks at the top as the omnipotent Creator, immune to change or imperfection; the highest being, who is perfectly good (Augustine 2013: III, 10). Then follow the angels, humans, animals, plants, and, further down, the rest of the lifeless universe. The more a thing is like its creator, in terms of being and goodness, the higher it ranks in the hierarchy of being. This is not unlike Plotinus's vision of the emanation of all things from God, where nearness and distance to the source determine the entities' being and goodness. There are, however, two decisive respects in which Augustine's thought breaks clearly with Plotinus's conception: first, for Augustine, there is a categorical – and not just gradual – distinction between Creator and creation. There is no outpouring of being, but an absolute act of creation *ex nihilo* (out of nothing). Second, for Plotinus, there is a notion of matter (*hyle*), which is furthest removed from the divine emanation and which is where evil resides. To Augustine, however, everything created is intrinsically good – including all matter – and where the entire order of creation is concerned, one must see that the totality of things is, indeed, "very good" (Gen. 1: 31; Augustine 2006: xviii; Hick 2010: 43–45). So how does evil creep in?

If evil does not stem from its own principle and is not an intrinsic quality of some matter, then, Augustine argues, it must come from a change within the good creation. The first premise for such conception of evil is that creation entails a separation between the changeless Creator and changeable beings. Having been created *ex nihilo*, the created being can change. However, both creation in its totality and each individual substance that is created are good, in the sense that they fill their place within creation, which means, for Augustine, that they exist according to their measure, form, and order. Since creation also contains change and freedom, though, perversion of measure, form, and order is possible – and, indeed, has become real (Augustine 2006: iii). For all rational creatures – angels and human beings – it is, more specifically, free will that makes change and perversion possible. Such perversion consists in a turn of the will from an orientation toward God to lesser things.

Evil is nothing but such a perversion – in twisting its order, the evil entity deprives itself of being and goodness. Evil is, according to Augustine's (2013: III, 11; 2003: XI, 21) famous phrase, the "privation of the good" (*privatio boni*). This privation does not mean that evil is simply the opposite of the good, because then, by definition, the good would be the opposite of evil – and thus the definition would be caught in a vicious circle, and would turn out to be empty. Moreover, Augustine is not suggesting that evil is merely an absence or an illusion. The point is, rather, that evil presupposes created goodness and becomes real only insofar as it corrupts or destructs creation. Although it may seem strange to us, Augustine just assumes – as his contemporary Neoplatonists assumed – that being and goodness are, essentially, one. This is perhaps not such a strange assumption as it seems, if one assumes that all beings are the creations of a good God. As God creates that which exists, he also creates it as being "very good," i.e., with inherent value. That which is lesser in the hierarchy of being is less good – and, along these lines, it becomes comprehensible that evil is not only not good, but it also does not even have being. Hence, as evil is a change from the good, it is also a movement toward destruction or nonbeing.

While evil corrupts goodness, Augustine argues, it can never become absolute evil, because then it would simply cease to exist. There is, therefore, an ontological asymmetry between goodness and evil: whereas good can exist autonomously, evil cannot. Evil cannot exist without good because evil is parasitic. In this way, the dualism between equal and rival forces is overcome, as the good being must take priority over the parasite that lives upon it. Augustine explains this relation thus:

> These two contraries are thus coexistent, so that if there were no good in what is evil, then the evil simply could not be, since it can have no mode in which to exist, nor any source from which corruption springs, unless it be something corruptible. Unless this something is good, it cannot be corrupted, because corruption is nothing more than the deprivation of the good. Evils, therefore, have their source in the good, and unless they are parasitic on something good, they are not anything at all. There are no other sources whence an evil thing can come to be. (Augustine 2013: IV, 14)

While the notion of evil as privation and parasite is truly an indispensable contribution to thinking on evil, this explanation has often been accused of being too passive: here, evil is characterized as an absence of goodness; a lack of being in its own right. When evil enters human affairs, it tends to have a clearly active dimension, such as in violence; even in the natural sphere, evil has a very real destructive character that does not immediately seem to fit the description of evil as privation. As Richard Swinburne (1998: 32) puts it: "pain is not just an absence of pleasure, and wicked acts are not just the non-occurrence of good acts." In Augustine's defense, it has been suggested that evil is like a vacuum, which demonstrates a pure lack but can have very concrete and pressing effects (Williams 2016: 91). Even if this explanation has something to it, though, some of the problems with Augustine's account have to do with the fact that the metaphysical backdrop of his thinking has lost its conviction, as seen in the hierarchy of being and the identity of being and the good. Both these motivate Augustine's idea of evil as *privatio boni*. A question remains, however, over whether it is possible to preserve the insight into evil as no thing, as parasitic and as evasive, without entering into Neoplatonic metaphysics.

A related problematic aspect of Augustine's account becomes clear when looking at what John Hick (2010: 82–85) has called Augustine's "aesthetic theme." What he has in mind is Augustine's tendency to justify the existence of evil via a grand outlook, where evil is regarded as analogous to an element of a great work of art. From this standpoint, every element of the work, even if not beautiful in itself, contributes to the overall beauty. When God declares His creation good, Augustine argues, God is not referring to individual entities; these entities are at higher and lower levels, are better or worse, and can stand in conflict with one another; they come together, nevertheless, to make up a harmonious totality. Darkness and contrast belong in a beautiful work of art. Despite the conflicting state of the things of the universe, Augustine (1992: VII, xiii, 19) concludes: "Yet with sounder judgement I held that all things taken together are better than superior things by themselves." In such a good totality, the problem becomes that evil tends to be figured as an aesthetic means to the end of completing a big picture, a position that renders each concrete instance of evil insignificant and effectively silences the voices of the victims – such as the lamenting and protesting Job.

Modern Versions

Theologian Karl Barth attempts to extend and revise central aspects of the Augustinian tradition through his notion of "nothingness" (*das Nichtige*). For Barth, no theological thought can take metaphysics or any other natural experience as its starting point. Given Barth's view regarding the limitations of human cognition where religious matters are concerned, knowledge can be imparted only by God Himself, in his self-revelation in Jesus Christ. Moreover, from the goodness revealed in Christ, Barth argues, we can gain insight into evil, in the sense of overcoming it, at least: God Himself becomes a vulnerable creature subjected to evil, who then defeats it from the inside. What this means for our understanding of evil is that there can be no denial of its existence because God Himself seeks to combat it. Indeed, evil stands opposed as much to the world as to God. Active resistance to God's world dominion is an alien factor that, although it is there, does not fit into creation; hence, Barth (1960: 289) terms it "nothingness."

Before grappling with the question of how this nothingness originated, Barth first delineates its essence – or, rather, anti-essence – in negative terms. As in Augustine, for Barth (1960: 292), nothingness cannot be explained by scrutinizing God's will, characterized by grace and love. Thus, there is no positive definition of evil, for it can be defined only through its very opposition with God's will. As for creation, Barth draws a decisive distinction: according to the story, God creates not only light but also night – or, more generally, not just a positive, but also a negative side. There is, in other words, a "shadowy side" to reality that must not be confused with nothingness, since it belongs to the good of creation, even when it does not appear as such at first glance. Good and bad days, youth and aging, birth and death are simply constitutive parts of human life and are not evil in themselves. If one mistakenly identifies the shadowy side with nothingness, Barth argues, one makes creation partly evil. Here, one both secretly refers nothingness back to the Creator and also fails to see its real destructiveness (Barth 1960: 299). It is not possible to explain nothingness through any criteria or measures available in the created world. All we can say about nothingness is what it is not – i.e., it is in strict opposition to the revealed God (Barth 1960: 302, 349).

Nonetheless, perhaps surprisingly, Barth has quite a bit to say about how nothingness has entered the scene. Both creation in general and God's covenant with His people more specifically rest on God's free and sovereign acts of election. In electing, God separates the creation that He wants from the chaos that He does not want. Nothingness also stems from God's activity: paradoxically, it comes into "existence" because God rejects it. It is not bestowed with existence as one of God's willed creations; rather, it exists solely to the extent that it is dismissed. According to Barth (1960: 351), the biblical account of creation has the following logic:

> God elects, and therefore rejects what He does not elect. God wills, and therefore opposes what He does not will. He says Yes, and therefore says No to that to which He does not say Yes. He works according to His purpose, and in so doing rejects and dismisses all that gainsays it. Both of these activities, grounded in His election and decision, are necessary elements in His sovereign action. He is Lord both on the right hand and on

the left. It is only on this basis that nothingness "is," but on this basis it really "is."

Nothingness, then, clearly falls on the side of the rejected, the No, the dismissed; that is, on what Barth calls God's "left hand." As with Augustine, nothingness has no existence, except in privation. Privation, in Barth's thinking, is not a passive lack but, rather, an active sense of opposing and destroying what exists. As the outcome of God's left hand, nothingness is not the object of God's proper intentions, which is grace. The grace that God aims to achieve is what He identifies as his own work (*opus proprium*), but, in enhancing this work, God is also active in confronting nothingness, which is the aim of his foreign work (*opus alienum*). The latter refers to the hidden side of God, where divine jealousy, wrath, and judgment come to the fore for the betterment of His creation. Nothingness is the target of the foreign work. As grace runs its course, according to the history of salvation, and the foreign work gradually fades, so too will nothingness, since it depends completely on being rejected.

Thus, Barth preserves the mysterious nonbeing of evil, while freeing it from Augustine's metaphysical framework. At the same time, Barth offers his own ideas about the emergence of evil. The attraction of his position stems from how he steers clear of the metaphysical integration of evil into either God or creation. However, it has its own questionable side. To speak of nothingness as coming into "being" through rejection appears to stretch our conceptions to breaking point. It seems rather more apt to say that things are brought forth by affirmation, not rejection, and so, to the extent that evil exists, it must exist despite God's creation. Barth seems to presuppose that something like nothingness must already be there in order for it to be rejected. But that would run counter to God's sovereign freedom in creating *ex nihilo*, a position to which Barth surely would not admit. As it stands, nothingness seems like a hypostatization of negation; God's "No," with a speculative ring to it.

Barth is in agreement with Augustine's privation theory, but has a clearer emphasis on the active, opposing force of nothingness. Yet one might wonder whether evil has a more intimate relationship with created things than that for which Barth allows. Is it not precisely because familiar things and persons can become destructive or violent that we take reality's evilness as uncanny – both homely and unhomely at the same time? Paul Tillich pursues this inner tension at the depth of things in a way that is very different from Barth's arguments. What he terms "demonic" is, however, not equated with nothingness. Tillich calls the latter "satanic": a pure, limited sense of the principle of negativity, without an existence of its own. For him, however, the satanic becomes an effective, destructive reality only when it participates in something that is given being, that is, as it becomes demonic. Tillich introduces his ideas in terms of the demonic depicted by "primitive people." Typically, demons are composed of well-known elements borrowed from the human, animal, or vegetative spheres, but they are combined in such ways that they shatter normal forms: plants growing on a human head with an animal body or the like. These combinations violate the overarching principle of created form and introduce a violent element that threatens unitary form from the inside (Tillich 1988: 100).

Tillich does stress that these natural elements are not evil in themselves; when their conflicts become overpowering, however, they disrupt form. The demonic, in Tillich's rendering, is not a lack or a nothing but, rather, something positive: the demonic is actively contrary to form. It is always within a formed being and cannot exist apart from it, just as Augustine and Barth claimed. Moreover, the importance of these observations is not restricted to "primitive art," for, according to Tillich, the truth they lay bare has dawned gradually on psychological researchers and modernist artists. Such observations, then, must be assumed to point to decisive tensions within human reality that are still givens today (Dahl 2015). In other words, according to Tillich, the realities we encounter have the same tension as found in primitive art: between that which preserves and encourages life, and an active, form-destroying element. The former is the divine principle, or grace, while the other is the demonic (Tillich 1988: 101).

From whence, though, does the demonic stem? Tillich makes no leap into the Heaven from which angels might fall, pointing neither to external sources nor to a lack of being or divine rejection. The demonic wells up from the same source as any created and creative element. In Tillich's ontology, all finite beings have form and ground, but they also have a root in the ungrounded, the abyss. To put it otherwise, being stands out from not-being. There is a depth in being that transcends all comprehension, and from this abyss, all concrete beings come into existence and gain form. This inexhaustible creative depth, however, contains its own dangers. As long as what wells up is integrated and in unity with form, things remain well. It can also work contrary to form, however, splitting it and turning it against itself, in which case, the demonic dynamic arises. There is a movement in the abyss that strives to break free from form altogether and bring about destruction (Tillich 1988: 103).

The advantages of making the demonic and destructive part of the experience of being, however, come with a price. There is a reason why Augustine and Barth struggle to keep evil distinct both from God and creation, to safeguard the goodness of God and the original goodness of creation. However, Tillich's proposal leaves us with the suspicion that, in the end, the tension and ambiguity that we find in creation can be traced back to God. Indeed, Tillich does not shy away from such a view. Rather, he argues that the demonic is overcome constantly within the movement of divine life itself (Tillich 1978: 246–247).

Evil As Suffering

One thing is strangely absent from the accounts I have presented so far, and that is human persons – both as agents and as sufferers. Both evil and God are depicted as abstract and depersonalized forces. However, evil is always concrete and comes to the fore in the acts or suffering of human beings. As for the God at stake, the monotheistic traditions have always insisted on speaking of God in narratives and using human metaphors. One way of putting it is to say that the accounts treated earlier have been occupied with metaphysical evil, that is, with imperfections and finitude, rather than moral evil.

It would, however, be wrong to say that moral evil escapes the attention of these traditions, given that sin – and, hence, moral evil – is one of the principal topics discussed at length elsewhere. Human nature itself is not evil but, rather, has a certain tendency to diverge from its proper orientation in life. Sin is, accordingly, not connected solely to evil actions, although it is manifest in them; rather, sin has roots deeper down, in a distorted relation to God, to oneself and to the world. Arguably, the doctrine of sin has been developed most profoundly in the Christian West, where the story of the fall has played a far more prominent role than in the Eastern Church, Judaism, and Islam. Indeed, the matter continues to inspire reflections within the Western tradition to the present day.

If one looks at evil from ancient mythological accounts up to modern philosophical and theological treatments, one can detect a growing tendency to place its root in human beings. At times, evil becomes almost synonymous with moral evil. For instance, Kant will speak of radical evil solely in relation to human morality. For him, evil is not metaphysical or natural, but is related to rational beings' tendency to prefer egoistic maxims or rules for their own conduct, at the expense of moral law (Kant 1960: 20–25; Bernstein 2002: 19–36). As early as Augustine's writings, the core of human evil has been considered located in the human will. For all their differences, Augustine, Barth, and Tillich all agree that sin is essential for understanding evil but that, nonetheless, evil cannot be fully reduced to sin; there is more to it. For some reason, evil has a place – or, rather, a non-place – in creation more broadly. In addition to the shrinking of the religious perspective that it entails, the concentration on moral evil also tends to focus on the active side – evil acts done – and to downplay evil undergone, experienced, and suffered passively. There have been more reflections on the motives, or lack thereof, of the perpetrators than on the experiences of the victims. For Job, this latter aspect of evil is central; more precisely, it is figured as innocent suffering. It is important to retain such a notion of the passive undergoing of evil because the world is full of experiences of illness, accidents, and frail dispositions – various forms of natural evil that are suffered without clear correlations with active agency or evil will. The world does not always – if ever – follow a moral order, and it is this conviction that Job will hold against his friends.

While leaving the topic of sin and suffering as discussed by Job and his friends for the next section, I suggest here that starting with individual suffering opens up a rather different perspective on evil. The perspective I propose here does not involve abstract, metaphysical discussions but stays close to the concrete way in which evil enters the body against one's will. Going back to Job, it is telling that Satan strikes twice: the first time he strikes, Job is robbed of all his property, servants, and children. Job keeps faithful, however, to his God: "the LORD gave, the LORD has taken away, blessed be the name of the LORD" (Job 1:21). Satan then suggests that if Job is hurt physically, things will change: "stretch out your hand now and touch his bone and his flesh, and he will curse you to your face" (Job 2:5). After this, Job is inflicted with some horrible skin disease, covering him with loathsome sores from the sole of his foot to the crown of his head (Job 2:7), and with blisters that harden and then break again (Job 7:5), making his skin turn black (Job 30:30).

The text does not have much interest in the nature of this disease, except in the sense that it makes Job suffer in an utterly concrete and physical way. The physical aspect of Job's pain has seldom been considered in any detail in the reception of the Book of Job, despite the fact that, once seen, it is manifest all over the text (Raz 2014). The pain that Job feels is not generalizable in the way that moral or metaphysical evil may be because pain singles Job out individually. Evil as pain is an individual experience to the point of utter isolation, something that is underscored by how Job feels cut off from the social milieu in general and from his friends in particular. The pain belongs inescapably to the individual; others remain sealed outside the experience (Scarry 1985: 4). Pain does not just single out Job's soul or personality; it becomes part of his very flesh. Job thus feels his incarnation to the point where he is locked up, constrained by his own skin.

Even if the sensation of pain itself remains notoriously hard to convey, the poetic sections of the Book of Job attempt to bring it out – especially by means of metaphors. The metaphor is a figure of speech that has one pole in sensation and another in the imaginative sphere. One of the root metaphors for pain repeated in various inflections throughout the Book of Job is that of being hit by an arrow. For instance, Job speaks of being set up as the target for God's archers (Job 16:12), and Zophar speaks of a bronze arrow that will strike him through (Job 20:24). This image conveys several important features regarding the suffering of pain (Dahl 2016: 47–48). First, it reflects the feeling of being so overcome by pain that it is as if one has been hit – an event over which Job, or anyone suffering pain, has no control and to which he is passively exposed. Being hit also implies someone aiming at Job – a someone who, in Job's case, can be identified as God. In this way, the metaphor captures how an experience of pain moves deeply into the self and thus feels like a personal offense. Second, the passivity of the self corresponds with being hit by an arrow from the outside. This "outside" does not mean the spatial outside, as Job is not, in fact, shot, but is afflicted by some kind of disease. Rather, it captures the way in which pain is always averse, unwelcome, something that should not be; it occurs contrary to, and hence outside, one's will and control. Third, the pain is as if an arrow is going right into the flesh – "for the arrows of the Almighty are in me," as Job puts it (Job 6:4). One of the characteristics of pain is that it is somatic, in an emphatic sense: if we tend to forget our own bodies when we watch, hear, or engage in something, pain, in contrast, makes our embodied beings present and impossible to ignore (Leder 1990: 74).

Emmanuel Levinas has shed light on both the exteriority of evil and its interiority. Starting with the latter, he notes that what makes physical pain real suffering is the impossibility of detaching oneself from it: it invades the body and becomes one with it, even as it remains averse to it. Thus, the sufferer is filled with the urge to flee this unwelcome guest, but to no avail: "In suffering there is an absence of refuge ... The whole acuity is made up of the impossibility of fleeing or retreating" (Levinas 1987: 69). Levinas points out that, as pain is an impression, just like color or warmth, it is received consciously into our interiority. However, unlike color and warmth, pain is not integrated into consciousness and therefore retains a certain exteriority. This exteriority is due to the excess by which pain is characterized; it is "too much" – not quantitatively, but qualitatively. It is unbearable because it opposes consciousness even as it invades it. The nature of the painful impression is such that it refuses any integration into experience, any unity of meaning; it is downright meaningless. Undergoing pain, therefore, is paradoxical: it is at once part of body and soul, and yet it refuses to become part of it. Just like the serpent, this evil does not belong anywhere fully. As it is felt and suffered, painful suffering is still "in the guise of 'experienced' content, the *way* in which, within a consciousness, the unbearable is precisely not borne, the manner of this not-being-borne; which, paradoxically, is itself a sensation or a datum" (Levinas 2006: 78).

Levinas thus argues that there is something inherent in the very experience of suffering that makes it evil: its resistance to consciousness and meaning, its negation, as a "not." Despite Levinas's penetrating phenomenological analysis of the basic manifestation of evil in painful suffering, it is important to add that, just as Barth warns us against identifying the "shadowy side" of creation with evil, so too must we acknowledge that there are types of pain that are not simply evil, even if they hurt. Indeed, there are pains that are productive in human life and development, such as the pain of growth. But such physical pains are not types of suffering associated with evil because they lend themselves to integration and to further meaning and purpose. When confronted with horrendous evils such as the Holocaust, which Levinas always keeps in mind, such a sense of purpose simply does not apply. Pain as evil, then, is meaningless, useless; it is "for nothing" (Levinas 2006: 79).

The Inexplicability of Evil

If one approaches evil in terms of the experience of pain, a somewhat different perspective is gained than that offered in the other accounts of evil discussed earlier. Such a perspective allows for no grand outlook from above, no "God's-eye view"; instead, it ushers us to start from below with the singular, isolated experience of being hit and wounded as an embodied being. Whether one starts from above or below, however, we are led to acknowledge the inexplicability of evil. Levinas finds this inexplicability embedded in the nature of pain itself: its resistance to integration into the unity of meaning. While starting from above, Augustine and Barth's accounts of evil also reach a point where evil's opaqueness and lack of meaning is emphasized. The meaninglessness at stake is not related to a meaning that has not yet been found, as in, let's say, a mathematical puzzle or a problem of interpretation; rather, in confronting us, the meaninglessness actively destroys meaning. In this way, Ingolf Dalferth (2006b: 3) sees evil not only as lacking meaning but also as going against meaning, breaking into life and its structures, bereaving it of its normal horizons of meaning and future.

For Augustine and Barth, the inexplicability stems from the internal logic of God's good creation: it is created good, yet evil is undeniably there. According to Augustine, looking for the causes of evil choices is like looking for something that does not exist. It is like trying to see darkness or hear silence. In both cases, we must use perceptual organs, although they do not really perceive what is absent. Augustine holds that there is no efficient cause for evil; there is only what he calls "deficiency." Augustine admits that we can gain some kind of knowledge of the evil will, but only as a specific way of not-knowing; there is no reason or cause behind it as it is simply perversion. We must learn, Augustine writes in a paradoxical passage, "not to know what must be known to be incapable of being known! For of course when we know things not by perception but by its absence, we know them, in a sense, but not-knowing, so that they are not-known by being known – if that is a possible or intelligible statement!" (Augustine 2003: XII.7). Only a sensitive manner of not-knowing, then, is apt for thinking about evil.

Here, Augustine touches on the limits of thought when the mind is faced with the mystery of evil. This is a central trope within theology generally, since the subject speaks of divine things from a finite perspective, even if the concept of revelation is granted. Such limits are also paramount for Barth's notion of theology, especially as he speaks of nothingness. Sin and evil cannot be fully grasped, for anything we can comprehend must accord with some norms or standards that are derived from our experiences of the world. But nothingness is precisely without such standards – it destroys them. Hence, "[b]eing hostile before and against God, and also before and against His creature, it [nothingness] is outside the sphere of systematization. It cannot even be viewed dialectically, let alone resolved" (Barth 1960: 354). Indeed, all theology is "broken theology" and cannot aspire to completeness, consistency, and totality, and this is precisely because nothingness is the very break that tears us apart from the original relation between God and humanity. What we can know, theologically speaking, can be granted to us only from above, and is received only via the condition of brokenness (Barth 1960: 293–294).

The opaque character of evil is preserved in both the perspective from above and the perspective from below. Reflecting on evil ends in aporia, in the unthinkable – namely, something destructive that should not be but, undeniably, is. Evil does not belong or fit in; not into our pre-reflective expectations of life and not into a religious or metaphysical perspective of creation. While both the perspective from above and the perspective from below reach this final conclusion, there are good reasons for giving priority to the perspective from below. Even if a focus on pain cannot exhaust all the dimensions of evil, it highlights a dimension that is otherwise easily neglected: that all talk about evil that does not relate to concrete human (or animal) experience must remain abstract. As Dalferth (2006a: 29) has argued, suffering does not comprise all thinkable forms of evil but is, nevertheless, the primary "place" in which evil becomes manifest in human life. As a phenomenon, evil must show itself, and it is revealed in human suffering, which is always undergone by individuals. This is another reason why the Book of Job offers an important occasion for reflecting on evil: Job maintains a perspective of evil that is directed strictly from below.

If there is no answer to the question of what evil is, one can easily come to feel that nothing is gained in thinking about it. However, an arrival at a broken state, at not-knowledge and the evasiveness of evil, also gives us deep insight. Ricoeur concludes his presentation of the history of the problem of evil with Barth's findings: what Barth came to see was that thinking about evil inevitably leads to aporia. Perhaps Barth can be taken, Ricoeur suggests, to have seen that the emphasis on non-contradiction and totality in the metaphysical tradition of the West has led to false theodicies. By leaving us with irreconcilable contradictions and impasses, such approaches to evil can provide us with a negative insight into the limits of human understanding and, from there, we can be led to "think more and otherwise" (Ricoeur 2007: 64).

Elements in Religion and Violence

2 Job's Friends: Theodicy

It seems that it is difficult to get one's head around the nature of evil, and the difficulty is not eased by thinking about the existence of evil together with the existence of a good, wise, and almighty Creator. Theodicy is the philosophical attempt to think through this difficulty, without laying the blame at God. "Theodicy" literally means justifying or defending God, and it arises as an apologetic response to the problem of evil. In its strict, rational sense, it is an eminently modern invention. The term was coined by Leibniz in his work from 1710, *Theodicy*, and its framework presupposes a certain stage of modernity. The very need to justify God's ways rationally can make full sense only against a background in which God is not taken as a given. In such a framework, reflecting on God and evil is no longer a method of searching for a more adequate understanding of the God that all believe in; rather, the search aims to give grounds for belief in God at all (Tilley 2000: 225–226). This situation is due to political and social transformations, the growth of human beings' autonomous self-understanding as rational agents, and the acceptance of the Newtonian universe governed not by divine will but by mechanical laws. That theodicy is modern in this sense does not mean, however, that it is entirely new; the problem of evil clearly has a long history stretching back to the Book of Job. What has changed, though, is that the burden of proof has shifted: the ultimate verdict regarding God's justice is not God's, but ours (Surin 1983: 226–228).

Job's Friends

The urge to defend God is manifest throughout the Book of Job. The book not only portrays an innocent victim of terrible suffering; it also depicts an array of responses to this situation. Indeed, there is a clear change in Job's own responses to his suffering, from his pious attitude in the prologue, via the lamenting and protesting Job of the dialogical part, to the quiet and repenting

Job toward the end (Buber 1969). The reactions of his friends are equally interesting, as they try to provide explanations for Job's suffering in various ways. Job certainly wants to know why God is letting him suffer, since he can see no reason for it. Job will not establish any kind of proto-theodicy; what he does is to protest. The development of such a proto-theodicy, however, becomes very much the task of his friends. Job breaks the silence after seven days and initiates the dialogue with his friends, as if the pain itself bursts out into a flow of expressions. He starts with a chapter-long discourse, cursing the day he was born and longing for his death (Job 3). Certainly, such self-expression is a cry for recognition and consolation. But, instead of consolation, his friends respond to him by providing possible explanations for his malady. As the dialogue unfolds, these explanations take form as rebukes, moralizations, and types of religious instruction. The three friends (if "friends" is the right word), Eliphaz, Bildad, and Zophar (and, later, the newcomer, Elihu), approach Job from different angles. Here, three recurring themes can be discerned.

First, the main point that the friends make repeatedly is that, despite appearances to the contrary, God's justice is indisputable. It guarantees that every person will receive his or her dues in the end: the righteous will get their reward and the wicked will be punished. Elihu puts it thus: "Far be it from God that he should do wickedness, and from the Almighty that he should do wrong. For according to their deeds he will repay them, and according to their ways he will make it befall them" (Job 34:11). In other words, a moral universe is presupposed, in which everything happens in accordance with divine Law. Hence, Job must either have some sins to confess, consciously or unconsciously performed, or else he is being punished for the sins of his ancestors. Either way, there is hope: if Job will only turn to God and repent, things will work out well for him (Job 5:8, 8:5–6). However, it is exactly this moral order of the world that has become unsustainable for Job; according to his own experience, there is simply no connection between justice and reward on this Earth. He has no reason to repent, and yet he suffers. Indeed, the wisdom literature in the Hebrew Bible, especially Job and Ecclesiastes, expresses a crisis in belief in the moral order and, hence, in the covenant: both texts observe a lack of consistency in the Law, seeing that the righteous and innocent suffer, while the wicked often prosper (Job 21:7; Eccles. 7:15).

Second, the friends point to the religious status of God. God is holy and pure, set apart from His creation, meaning that no creature can approach God without facing utter peril. So, even prior to any moral charge of misdeeds or sin, anyone born of woman is inherently impure and unfit to draw near to God. As Eliphas rhetorically asks: "Can mortals be righteous before God? Can human beings be pure before their Maker?" (Job 5:17). This general outlook is sharpened in the case of Job, since Job addresses his complaints and protests directly to God and thus, according to Zophar, profanes his holiness – Job even mocks God with his declaration of his own purity (Job 11:4).

The third strand of arguments is related to the second in its appeal to the impossibility of finite beings understanding God. "Can you find out the deep things of God?" (Job 11:7) Zophar asks rhetorically, referring to our limited access to God, who is above Heaven and beneath the underworld. Just as God transcends and withdraws from human understanding, God will also be frightening and sublime when He chooses to show Himself. This is because His power and might are immensely mightier than that which we can take in; hence, no human reason or response can be adequate in the face of His transcendence (Job 37:1–5). Such an image of the transcendence of God, figured as hidden or sublime, is the only insight that Job and his friends seem to agree on (Job 28:12–14). However, the positions from which such an insight is reached differ significantly. The friends works primarily to reduce the unrelenting Job to silence, demonstrating that his accusations and claims are in vain and that their own accounts are warranted. For Job, however, the hiddenness of God is an insight bought at the price of experiencing how his previous image of God falls to pieces.

Interestingly, the proto-theodicies of the friends already have some of the traits that will characterize the later versions of theodicy. They attempt to make some sense of evil not by taking the nature of concrete suffering into account, but by attempting to find theories or schemes that account for why God would allow suffering in general.

Augustine and Irenaeus

In the West, there is a distinct history of apologies for God's ways with the world, which can be traced from the early Church Fathers to our own time. In order to sketch out some of the significant phases within this history, I present a handful of important contributions from different stages in time that also suggest the major strategies still followed today.

In the previous section, I visited Augustine's view of the nature of evil. Augustine also has quite a few things to say about how evil enters God's creation. To put it in a more Augustinian manner, the question is not only "What is the nature of evil?" as explored in the previous section, but also "Wherefrom does evil come?" Deeply engrained in Augustine's (1992: I, xx, 31) piety is the conviction that all the good that befalls one and all the good deeds that one performs are received from God. It is not so, however, with evil, because evil does not flow from above but seems to have its roots in each of us. From these observations, we can already see the point: God is free of the charge of originating evil. Similar claims have been made in more recent times within analytical philosophy by such thinkers as Alvin Plantinga (1971) and Richard Swinburne (1998), in what they call "the free-will defense," arguing that human freedom comes at the price of the possibility and actuality of moral evil.

In order to ensure that his argument is in keeping with biblical traditions, Augustine must be able to trace the connection between the present sinful state of humanity and the biblical account of its origins. This makes sense, especially in terms of the turn toward moral evil – or sin, as Augustine terms it – as even when someone makes a bad decision or performs a harmful act by free will, the sin does not start with his or her conduct. It has already been operative in previous generations before it became inherited by the person in question. If we inquire into this tradition, eventually, we are led back to the story of Eden, in which the first human beings turn from God toward evil. The story of the fateful apple and the fall not only describes the origin of the human propensity for sin but also includes natural evils such as death, pain, and hardship (Gen. 3:15–19). However, going back to this account merely postpones the question. For how could the good creations of God, Adam and Eve, choose to act against the Creator's will if they were placed in a perfect harmonious relation with Him and lived according to His will? Augustine makes clear that Adam and Eve should not be considered evil by nature, for, as we have seen, everything created is, by definition, good. The decisive factor, according to Augustine, is not created nature, but the will. It is free will alone that can turn away from the highest good – God – and direct itself toward the lower (Augustine 2003: XII, 3). This downward orientation is the essence of sin. Thus, for Augustine, the free will can turn, even though there is no reason for it – no rational explanation and nothing causing it, simply an inexplicable perversion.

But, again, how could the impulse for such perversion enter the state of Eden? The question pushes for a further regression and an examination of the figure of the serpent, which Augustine interprets as the mouthpiece of the fallen angel. Augustine (2003: XIV, 11) asserts that the fallen angel had a motive for tempting humans to fall – namely that, since he himself had fallen, he became envious of non-fallen humans. The serpent's temptation must, Augustine argues, have appealed somehow to Adam and Eve, and awakened a slumbering desire to become gods themselves – hence, they gave in to the serpent's temptation. But then how did the angel fall in the first place?

Augustine embarks on lengthy discussions about this particularly difficult and, to him, decisive fall. The angels, partaking in the bliss of God and without sensual bodies to tempt them, should not have any disposition to fall. There is no rival principle that has driven them, such as Manicheism claimed, and God would certainly not have given them cause to turn away from Him (Augustine 2003: XI, 13–15). So, again, it must be a perversion of the will – or, to be more precise, a matter of pride:

> When we ask the cause of the evil angels' misery, we find that it is the just result of their turning away from him who supremely is, and their turning towards themselves, who do not exist in that supreme degree. What other name is there for this fault than pride? "The beginning of all sin is pride." . . . In preferring themselves to him, they chose a lower degree of existence. (Augustine 2003: XII, 6)

The angels were driven out of Heaven by their own choice, turning toward the lower – that is, toward themselves – in pride. Pride lies at the heart of all sin and spreads from the fallen angels to the first human beings, throughout history and up to our present state of sin. This is not God's doing, Augustine argues, but is due to free will. In this account of the justification for God (theodicy), then, God is deemed free from any charges and the blame is placed on humanity.

Augustine renders the myth of the fall, in Heaven and on Earth, in a rational way. He speculates about what went on among the angels, far beyond biblical accounts, and he treats the story of Eden as if it were a historical origin for sin. Taking the story of Eden as historical, he develops the theory of transmission of sin through sexual intercourse, which is highly problematic. However, the legitimate insight that Augustine wants to convey is the unconditional state of sin in which everyone finds himself or herself, a state that is neither chosen nor possible to flee by one's own means. But in explaining such a condition through a mixture of ethical and biological notions of heredity, he ends up claiming that both sin and guilt become part of one due to reproduction, i.e., independent of any actions on one's own part. I believe, however, that the logic of myths does not allow for such explanations: myths are neither rational nor irrational, but are illuminating only in accordance with their own mythical logic. Augustine does not consider this logic and its limitations sufficiently by, for instance, giving us a detailed account of what took place in Heaven among the angels before and during the fall, or of Satan's motive for seducing Eve. Put simply, myths are edifices unfit to uphold Augustine's rational constructions (Ricoeur 2004: 276).

The story of human sin in Augustine and the Latin-speaking part of the Church tended to look back at the perfect state of harmony and integrity from which the first human beings fell. However, even at the time, a competing story was already told among the Greek-speaking Church Fathers. Here, the view was more forward-looking. Adam and Eve were taken to represent not a lost state of perfection, but a state of immaturity (Hick 2010: 237). One of the first Church Fathers, Irenaeus of Lyon, claimed that it follows analytically from the concept of creation that human beings are made lower than God; as He is uncreated, God is perfection, the ultimate cause and principle behind all that is. As created beings, humans are in an imperfect state from the beginning; they are children who need to grow toward perfection (Irenaeus 2016: IV, xxxviii, 1). To capture this dynamic aspect of growth, Irenaeus introduces a distinction that he finds operative in Genesis: between humans as "images" of God (which we already are by means of creation) and as "likenesses" of God – i.e., human perfection, the ultimate goal. Maturation stands at the center of human history: starting out childlike, humanity must grow and evolve, be healed from sin through Christ, and eventually reach the likeness of God (Irenaeus 2016: IV xxxviii, 3). Irenaeus does not deny that we are created free and responsible, even if both freedom and responsibility increase as humanity develops. Our freedom consists of one fundamental choice – either to obey God through our own efforts or to refuse to do so – and to take the just divine punishment for that. Even faith is a matter of will in Irenaeus's account because it is only as a result of personal will that faith truly becomes our own (Irenaeus 2016: IV, xxxviii, 1, 5).

Note, though, that, despite all the emphasis Irenaeus places on freedom, he does not offer some kind of Augustinian free-will defense, placing all the responsibility for evil on human shoulders. Indeed, Irenaeus does not back down from the conviction that God is responsible for making both angels and humans open to pursuing evil instead of goodness. Why? According to Irenaeus, if goodness were fixed in our natures, it would destroy our sense of goodness and our desire for reunion with God. Goodness is pursued and held precious only insofar as it is not simply a given; it is something that one must attain. In this sense, Irenaeus holds that evil in the world does serve a function: as evil creates resistance to achieving the good, the desire for the good is increased. Thus earthly travails are necessary in order to fully appreciate the joy of God's kingdom:

> Moreover, the faculty of seeing would not appear to be so desirable, unless we had known what a loss it were to be devoid of sight; and health, too, is rendered all the more estimable by an acquaintance with disease; light, also, by contrasting it with darkness; and life with death. Just in the same way is the heavenly kingdom honorable to those who have known the earthly one. (Irenaeus 2016: IV, xxxvii, 7)

In short, evil is part of the world in which we live and, being so, evil can serve the divine pedagogics that, with the help of God, will lead humans to achieve the likeness of God.

It could be argued that, if Augustine rationalizes myths in order to construct grand metaphysical perspectives, he loses touch with concrete suffering along the way. Meanwhile, in Irenaeus's thought, although there are no metaphysical attempts to envisage the static unity of the universe, there is a grand view of the unity of the history of salvation. Within this perspective, evil is a necessary part of historical growth toward perfection – for individuals no doubt, but ultimately for humanity. The obvious problem is that the countless victims who suffer for no reason are rationalized as pedagogical means that make the historical wheel turn. Hence, the key question: do Augustine and Irenaeus really take evil seriously – as evil?

Modern Theodicy

By making a historical jump to the eighteenth century, we meet with theodicy proper, against the backdrop of modern enlightenment and rationalism. Even if God's existence, goodness, power, and wisdom cannot be taken for granted as metaphysical givens any longer, the basic questions are the same: How can there be a good and almighty God, given all the evil in the world? Why does the world contain so much suffering? And, more specifically, could God not have made a better world? From Leibniz's metaphysical standpoint, imperfections such as evil do not suddenly creep into the world, but follow analytically from creation. Being created, the world is separated from its perfect Creator and must, therefore, be imperfect. Thus Leibniz (2017: 92) holds that it is necessary that the created world, however it was made, contains some degree of metaphysical evil (finitude), physical evil (suffering), and moral evil (sin). In line with classical theism, Leibniz claims that we know that the Creator is good, so God must have made things for the best for us; we know that He is wise, so He will have chosen the best option for us, just as we know that He is powerful and so was able to bring such a world into existence.

Leibniz presupposes the Platonic thought that God has an infinite intellect of ideas. While having ideas about an infinite number of worlds that He could create, He chose to create ours, even if it contained evil. How could a good and wise God do that? Leibniz's (2017: 86) answer is simply that He chose the best of all possible worlds – and must have done so by definition, since He is good: "Now this supreme wisdom, united to a goodness that is no less infinite, cannot but have chosen the best. For as lesser evil is a kind of good, even so a lesser good is a kind of evil if it stands in the way of greater good; and there would be something to correct in the action of God if it were possible to do better." In other words, the kinds of evil are as limited as possible because the good, wise, and almighty God has created the best of all possible worlds.

What most readers react to immediately in Leibniz's theodicy is his very take on the problem of evil. Leibniz proceeds as if the problem of evil is a mathematical puzzle that needs a solution. He offers definitions and deductions to pursue his argument toward its conclusion. Leibniz professes at once to know too much and too little. He knows too much in terms of rational insight into the divine point of view, for how does Leibniz actually know that our world is the best? The answer seems to rest on a circular argument. He knows it is the best because God is good, and he knows that God is good because He chose the best of all possible worlds. But no human experience can possibly affirm that ours is the best, for we lack any ability to make a comparison with other worlds. At the same time, Leibniz knows too little about the victims of evil – or more precisely, it is not knowledge that he lacks, but proper acknowledgment of the evil of human suffering. If we live in the best of worlds, then evil should not bother us – no consolation, no protest, no hope for better times, but simply toughminded acceptance of how things are. That vision, however, will lead one either to despair or to cynicism.

Moreover, the "best of worlds" theory is very hard to uphold once one is struck by actual, lived suffering. Of course, one can question the sufferer's authority to comment on matters like this by claiming that any honest philo-sophizer must be free to explore theodicy. The discussion concerning theodicy far from ends with Leibniz; it is still going strong, especially within Anglo-American analytic philosophy. Since more recent theodicies follow in the wake of the accounts already mentioned, it suffices here to point to a few important contributions. John Hick revitalizes the tradition of Irenaeus, making a strong case for the necessity of evil in order to foster "soul-making," that is, the development of cherished character traits such as compassion, integrity, truth-fulness, and love. Evolution testifies that we are not heirs to a couple living in perfection, as Hick points out, but are the outcome of a long process, in which growth and maturation develop through resistance and hardship. If we were to imagine a "better world" than ours, one that lacks pain and suffering, we would see that those essential human traits would not be fostered. So God must have had good reasons for creating the world the way it is, including all evil, and it is through those evils that, ultimately, He steers the world toward a promised eschatological resolution (Hick 2010: 306–308, 362–364).

Rather than following Irenaeus, Richard Swinburne prolongs the Augustinian tradition, arguing for a free-will defense. Generally speaking, Swinburne contends that there are good reasons for God to allow bad things to happen – not because God is evil, but because those bad things are necessary means enabling the attainment of greater goods. Swinburne considers freedom to be one of those supreme goods, which means that in creating free agents, God must let them choose between good and bad. All the consequences of the bad decisions are, according to Swinburne, justified in the sense that they are risks that God cannot prevent in creating agents with genuinely free will (Swinburne 1998: 127). In line with Hick, Swinburne argues that hardship and pain are bad, but they are necessary conditions for fostering good character traits, such as responsibility, sympathy, and courage. Indeed, in denying a bad state, one is, in effect, removing the condition of cherished goods. God is justified in allowing evil to occur as long as the goodness outweighs the bad, and if we also take into account the compensation in the life to come, the balance turns out right. Hence, God is justified for allowing the evils of this world (Swinburne 1998: 239).

Many analytic philosophers have come to speak of "defense" rather than "theodicy." Typically, a defense will no longer claim to know the truth of God's reason for allowing evil, but will rather, more modestly, raise possible responses that at least make God compatible with the existence of evil. The argument does not pretend to be issued from God's position in a courtroom, but simply to defend a Theist's position over against an Atheist's charges in front of a neutral, agnostic jury. Negatively, the defense aims at undermining the charge and, positively, in telling a plausible story that makes the case convincing (van Inwagen 2008: 7, 65–66; Stump 2012: 18–20). Peter van Inwagen's defense agrees with the Augustinian tradition: only the free-will defense can stand up against the argument from evil, particularly because arguments against it fail. But whereas such a defense works where the global question of the existence of evil is at issue, it has little to offer when it comes to local cases: Why is a school bus crushed by a landslide? Why must a child be born without limbs? Why could not God prevent such specific states of affairs? First, van Inwagen contends, God cannot rule out every bad state, because they are necessary in order for humans to understand their self-imposed estrangement from God and hence to seek their way back to Him. Still, we might assume that God prevents many bad states or events. The question is why God draws the line between those He prevents and those He allows to happen – it simply appears arbitrary. Van Inwagen argues that such arbitrariness is justified. It is like having medicine only for 999 out of 1,000 seriously sick children: it should be used, even though one child must be left without treatment (van Inwagen 2008: 105–111). Such a reply raises deeply disturbing existential and theological issues, but the fact that van Inwagen focuses on local evil is helpful. Although he does not dwell on the nature of concrete manifestations of evil, at least he takes it as a point of departure for his arguments against arguments from local evil. Van Inwagen thereby makes clear that defenses or theodicies that solely deal with the problem of evil on a global level fail to discuss a very important dimension of evil.

For all their argumentative rigor, some feel that these contemporary theodicies and defenses leave us cold in their treatment of what is otherwise taken as burning issues. There is huge difference between Job's passionate complaints and the argumentative, even calculating attitude that some have called a "kind of religious utilitarianism" (Phillips 2004: 108–109). Van Inwagen readily admits that his story hardly comforts the victim, but adds that "the purpose of the story is not to comfort anyone" (van Inwagen 2008: 108). Neither Hick, Swinburne, nor van Inwagen regards his philosophical task as to care for the victim, but rather to test and put forth possible arguments. The question, then, is whether the distance to real suffering and evil is the best way to obtain the desired clarity of the arguments, or if such philosophy rather obscures the motivation for thinking about evil in the first place. Arguing the latter, Rowan Williams claims that much modern theodicies and defenses appear as evasions. If theodicy is not a response to those who suffer evil, then for whom is theodicy? In whose presence is theodicy carried out? Williams (2007: 273) replies: "If the answer to this is, 'In the absence of the sufferer as subject or narrator,' how can it fail to evade – to evade not only humanity, but divinity as well?"

3 Job's Response: Anti-Theodicy

Many of the arguments presented by theodicists, both ancient and modern, seem perfectly clear and consistent as they stand, and yet they provoke reluctance. But where does the reluctance toward theodicy stem from? The aim of what has been given the label "anti-theodicy" is to find a way to articulate that reluctance and to turn it in alternative directions. In a strict sense, the notion is obviously parasitic to "theodicy" – and if the latter is of a modern making, then so is anti-theodicy. Although the term has come to be used more commonly in recent decades, Kant's essay "On the Miscarriage of All Philosophical Trials in Theodicy" (2001) can be regarded as one of the earliest expressions of anti-theodicy. While Kant takes pains to rebut the most important arguments put forward in theodicy, he also gives expression to an overarching criticism of the project as such. In more recent times, anti-theodicy has become not so much a matter of refuting theodicists' arguments, even if some writers do that too; rather, principally, the purpose has been to criticize the very presuppositions behind the kinds of rational arguments and explanations made in relation to evil in the first place (Pihlström 2013: 130). As is the case with theodicy, the roots of anti-theodicy originate in the distant historical past. Indeed, Job's own reactions toward his friends serve as an appropriate starting point for understanding the motivations from which anti-theodicy developed.

Job Against His Friends

The long poetic section of the Book of Job is modeled as a dialogue – a genre possibly borrowed from Babylonian literature (Seow 2013: 66). As it unfolds, however, it turns gradually into a broken dialogue in which no mutual recognition and learning take place. Job and his friends go on to exchange views for some time, even if it becomes evident that they are speaking past one another. The parties grow impatient and then become overtly angry with one another, turning to ad hominem attacks or losing interest altogether in what is being said (Job 12:3, 15:6, 19:2). According to Job, the friends do not listen. Here is a man troubled with sorrow and shouldering unbearable pain, trying to reach out. Naturally, he is plagued by the difficulty of self-expression that anyone in pain knows about: it is hard to put the silent experience into adequate words. Thus, he is in need of someone to welcome those words: to meet them not with explanations and theories, but with compassion and understanding. In the main, the lack of dialogical recognition is not due to the topics that the friends address, for Job agrees that justice, the moral universe, the observance of the Law, and the transcendence of God are the topics at stake. The fact that they agree on the issues at hand would, in normal circumstances, be sufficient for a dialogue between differing opinions to take place.

The gulf between Job and his friends is not due, therefore, to the content of the conversations; rather, it is related to the attitudes expressed in the various speech acts. The friends converse with Job, but they speak in an abstract manner that fails to address his state of suffering. After a while, Job becomes weary of replying to his friends, turning toward God instead. This change of direction not only underlines the breach in human communication about suffering; it also reflects Job's conception of God as a distant, yet also intimate, interlocutor. Unlike his friends, Job refuses to speak simply *about* God; he also speaks *to* God. "I would speak to the Almighty," Job says, and goes on a little later to do so: "withdraw your hands from me, and do not let dread of you terrify me. Then call, and I will answer; or let me speak, and you reply to me" (Job 13:3, 21–22). Talking about God, as in the proto-theodicy of Job's friends, entails that God is treated as an object within a theoretical framework, whereas talking *to* God is a direct address to a personal God. In the latter case, there will be expressions that are confessions and complaints, and the expectation of a response; no explanations, however, have any proper place here. The implications of the speech act are altogether different (Burrell 2008: 17–19).

What torments Job is not the lack of a credible theodicy, but the lack of response from his divine interlocutor. The pain Job experiences still requires a response from God, who seems to stay behind the arrow He has fired. Since

Job's exceptional case – that of the innocent sufferer – does not fit into the schemes of his friends; he has lost confidence in the worldly, dogmatic, or metaphysical explanations that seek to make suffering an outcome of a retributive justice. The God he conceives goes beyond all such schemes. He can accept a response only from God Himself, and one that reveals both who God is and who Job himself is in relation to God. Waiting for God's response puts Job in a state of constant wavering between bitterness and despair, confidence and hope (Job 19:6–7, 25–26). For better or worse, he wants the matter settled urgently: "How many are my inequities and my sins? Make me know my transgression and my sin. Why do you hide your face, and count me as your enemy?" (Job 13:22–24). Job cannot come to see what he is charged with; he has committed no particular sin that deserves a punishment like this. On the contrary, he claims, he has acted justly all his life. Indeed, Job is ready to defend his integrity and innocence, even if it will cost him his life, for even the harshest of judgments is still a reply and as such, an acknowledgment.

It is not wrong to regard the Book of Job as one of those classical writings on the problem of evil – in some ways, it certainly is. What is a mistake, however, is to consider the text an example of theodicy. Theodicy is present as an important theme in the Book of Job, but it is not found in the mouth of Job; rather, it is voiced by his opponents, his so-called friends. A more adequate reading, therefore, entails interpreting Job not as providing arguments against theodicy, but as displaying how theodicy fails. In other words, the book can be read as deconstructing the enterprise of theodicy (Burrell 2008: 123–124). That a justification of God is not the moral of the story is emphasized further by the fact that not even God, in his theophany, tries to defend himself against Job's charges (Seeskin 2000: 67). For Kant, theodicy is based on arguments more scandalous than the charge from which they seek to protect God. Kant flags what have remained the main objections to theodicy ever since: first, that it falls short of morality in one way or another (outlined, for Kant, by the contrast with Job's integrity and sincerity), and, second, that it disregards the negative insight of the limits of human knowledge in speculating about things that, in both Kant's and Job's words, are "too high for us" (Kant 2001: 230, 232; Job 42:3). Let me turn to both these objections in turn, starting with the one concerning morality.

Anti-Theodicy and Moral Sensitivity

The most weighty charge against theodicy is that its theoretical discussions eclipse the moral dimension of evil. According to Terrence W. Tilley, a common presupposition among classical and contemporary theodicists is a detached point of view, which is well suited in relation to metaphysical or historical panoramas. Of course, such accounts are seldom designed to console or inspire action but, rather, to be purely theoretical and non-practical in nature. Tilley (2000: 231) argues that the world as described from such a detached point of view quickly becomes an idealized version, in which all the messy elements of joy and suffering are leveled out, and practical implications and political ideologies are ignored. However, he believes that such a problematic position is revealed most clearly if we regard these sorts of explanations as performative utterances and consider what the words do and imply when used. And, following Tilley, the outcome is that those utterances reduce the voices of the victims to silence. But what about Job? Does his story not contain theoretical outlooks too? In Tilley's reading, this is not the case. Using speech act theory, Tilley argues that the Book of Job is purposefully self-defeating as the depictions of God, revelation, and compensation fail to meet any meaningful standards. Regarded as a performative utterance, the Book of Job as a whole can be seen as solely negative. The performance becomes simply a warning, both against the friends' theodicy and against the elaboration of sadomasochistic pictures of

God (Tilley 2000: 109). To Tilley, this warning is an important teaching with critical potential, which can be turned against what he regards as the self-blinding and immoral project of theodicy.

As I argue in Section 4, however, there is more to Job's vision of God than simply a warning against perverted pictures of God. For now, though, it suffices to say that the main upshot of Tilley's account is that theodicy complies with upholding evil in the world, partly by ignoring cases of individual suffering and partly by neglecting critical perspectives on repressive social structures. Sami Pihlström also rejects theodicy with some of the same vigor, albeit along other philosophical avenues – employing not speech act theory, but pragmatism. When evil is discussed on an abstract and purely theoretical level, Pihlström argues, the first fatal step has already been taken. Consequently, there is no need to go into a discussion of details to counter theodicy, since the entire project moves in the wrong direction from the outset. In their joint book on theodicy, Pihlström and Kivistö (2016: 4) state that "theodicies fail to adequately recognize or acknowledge the meaninglessness of suffering and typically treat suffering human beings ... as mere means to some alleged overall good." This lack of acknowledgment includes the suffering individual, his or her experience, and the corresponding expressions of suffering. In short, theodicy fails to address the reality of suffering. Note that they do not have the work of particular philosophers in mind here but, rather, they criticize the tendency to deny and excuse the evil – a tendency that inhabits all of us (Pihlström and Kivistö 2016: 6). Just as Tilley, Pihlström, and Kivistö argue, the problem is not only that theodicy overlooks this aspect but also that it sustains radical evil.

Such an accusation regarding a radical evil draws on the legacy of Kant, in whose work "radical" refers to the root of evil within human beings. As mentioned earlier in this Element, Kant sees the human propensity for drawing toward evil as consisting of the prioritization of one's own welfare at the expense of following the imperatives of moral law. What this often comes down to is the human tendency of using others as means to an end, not as an end in themselves. From such a perspective, it is not difficult to understand here how Augustine's speech on the harmonious whole, Irenaeus's progressing history, and Hick's "soul making" can be seen as based on making others' suffering into a means to reach a higher good.

Such structures of radical evil are also reflected in the Book of Job. Pihlström and Kivistö regard the friends as proponents of theodicy and Job as the relentless defender of what Kant calls "moral sincerity." Despite the friends' explanations for the causes of Job's torment and even the revelation of God's might beyond understanding, Job stands tall. Kant, along with Pihlström and Kivistö, believes that Job can be seen as justified precisely because he does not give up faith in morality. The theodicy of his friends, in contrast, is deemed evil because it is morally insincere and lacking in integrity (Kant 2001: 232–233; Pihlström and Kivistö 2016: 44).

At this juncture, I pause to ask if it is really wrong, immoral, or even evil to respond theoretically to the problem of evil, as the anti-theodicists claim. Of course, no one claims that theodicists such as Hick, van Inwagen, Plantinga, and Swinburne are more immoral or evil than other people. They will regard their philosophical and theological contributions as set apart from moral and religious life – as operating on their own theoretical premises. To thinkers like Hick, accusing theodicists of impiety for a lack of sensitivity to agonizing suffering comes to nothing because practicing theodicy is doing nothing more than pursuing the intellectual vocation that is entailed in all philosophical and theological thinking. The practical and experiential problem of suffering, he argues, remains distinct from the work of thinking about it (Hick 2010: 6–10). There seems to be some truth in this. Still, it is precisely the split between philosophy and other aspects of life that anti-theodicists will question.

Anti-Theodicy and the Limits of Sense

The second strand of theodicy criticism, according to Kant, concerns the point that theodicy typically disregards the limitations of human understanding. One of the standing objections – often expressed without further argument – is that theodicy is somehow wrong because it is abstract. But, of course, all philosophy entails abstraction, otherwise it would not be able to deal with the most general dimensions of reality. However, the charge of abstraction is given more credence when it is contrasted with the concreteness of evil. Yet it can only take on full philosophical force if such abstraction can be shown to transgress our very conditions for intelligibility and, hence, makes accounts of the matter void and meaningless. In the wake of Kant, philosophers have turned to the conditions of the possibility of knowledge in order to delineate the scope and limits of knowledge in general. The aim here has been to safeguard knowledge and criticize unfounded conceptions. According to Kant (1929: 7, 56), it is only thus that one can hope to rid oneself of the illusions that one is led toward due to a certain metaphysical drift with which humanity seems to be burdened – more precisely, the human tendency to raise questions that we cannot possibly answer.

The conditions of the possibility of knowledge do not have to be conceived of, though, in terms of Kant's intuition and categories. In the past 100 years, these conditions have been recast repeatedly in relation to practices, social formations, and, not least, language. Like Kant before him, Ludwig Wittgenstein argued that the life we lead with words at once conditions us as intelligible creatures and makes us harbor deep impulses to transgress the meanings of these words; we seek either to reach a kind of crystalline clarity of logic, a metaphysical foundation, or an unmediated grasp of reality. To come to acknowledge what we can, in fact, meaningfully mean is what Wittgenstein calls for. He does so by providing reminders of how we use ordinary language.

For him, it is by reflecting patiently on the web of ordinary speech and activities that we can trace the grammar of words – that is, comprehend their proper roles within language games. The aim here, in Wittgenstein's (2009: § 116) terms, is to "bring words back from their metaphysical to their everyday use." Clearly, such a return of words can be applied to religious concepts too.

D. Z. Phillips has brought the ambitions of Wittgenstein's philosophy to bear on the problem of evil, not in order to offer any explanation but to elucidate its possible meaning, while, at the same time, recognizing the limits of sense. Phillips is also very critical of theodicy as it is deployed in contemporary analytical philosophy. He finds repeatedly that different theodicies neglect the limits of meaning and the ways in which words are governed in religious lives. They entail a certain hubris: "Theodicies," Phillips (1993: 153) writes, "are an extreme example of the philosophical reluctance to accept that there may be something beyond human understanding." One example of such reluctance comes to expression in discussions of omnipotence. As I pointed out in the introduction, God's omnipotence is, along with perfect goodness and the existence of evil, the premise that generates the trilemma of evil. But what does it mean that God is omnipotent? At first glance, it seems that an omnipotent God must have unlimited power to do whatever He wants. On closer scrutiny, however, the matter is a little more complicated. Swinburne (1998: 3) offers this definition:

> An omnipotent being is one who can do anything logically possible, anything, that is, the description of which does not involve a contradiction: such a being could not make me exist and not exist at the same instant, but he could eliminate the stars or cover the earth with water just like that.

Admittedly, then, there are logical constraints to God's omnipotence, but those are not limitations of power; rather, they are limitations laid down by logic.

This logical definition is made independently of the religious – say, biblical – understanding of God's power and, according to Swinburne, could thus be applied to any being, in principle.

But here the problems commence, for underlying the account is a conviction that logic determines sense independently of the context of its application. That, however, is a conviction that Wittgensteinians such as Phillips most strongly oppose: the logic or sense of a word is not an inner property or a fixed point of reference but is determined solely by the role that words occupy in a context embedded in a form of life. To rob the logic of that context is to render it meaningless and empty. Phillips (2004: 12) illustrates the arbitrariness of making abstract logic that determines what God can or cannot do with the following examples: without contradiction, God must be able to do such things as "riding a bicycle, licking and savouring a Häagen-Dazs ice-cream, bumping one's head, having sexual intercourse, learning a language and so on." This is Phillips's way of pointing out that discussions about God's omnipotence such as that provided by Swinburne simply fail to make the kind of sense they are supposed to. By showing that such definitions of omnipotence lead to absurd consequences, the point is not to banish talk of an almighty God from religious life; on the contrary, the idea is to show how philosophizing stops making sense as soon as one forgets how religious words are used in religious life. Thus, the alternative to abstract logic is to look at how words are practiced in the contexts in which they belong – for example, in worship or liturgy. It is through investigating the context that one can hope to detect the grammar of "the almighty God" (Phillips 2004: 114).

There is a strong inclination to employ concepts derived from religious contexts as materials for scientific explanation. Miracles, for example, are often regarded as a violation of natural laws, but that is hardly how biblical implications of Jesus's miracles take on meaning. Phillips argues that religious orientation is not based on scientific hypotheses but on ways to respond to the contingencies of our human life. Questions and responses have other directions and points than scientific explanations. Suppose there was an earthquake and it could be fully explained by geologists. Such explanations would not be of any help to a woman who has lost her house and child. Her "Why?" would not await any such scientific explanations, and perhaps no explanations at all – and certainly not some sort of philosophical super-explanation that encompasses all sciences (Phillips 2004: 131). Something of the same point is made in Phillips's comments on the Book of Job. The book, of course, raises many difficult questions, but in Phillips' (2004: 121) reading, Job displays no urge to go beyond the limits of what can be meaningfully known:

> Job is silent when asked, "Where wast thou when I laid the foundations of the Earth? Declare, if thou hast understanding" (Job 38:4). Not so our present day theodicists. In effect, their books and articles reply: "It is true that we were not there, and that you haven't exactly given us full details, but we know exactly what it must have been like and why you did it."

Phillips has made a strong case regarding the limits of what theodicy can claim, but one might wonder whether he makes things too easy for himself. For all the apt criticism of the emptiness of some of the conclusions drawn, theodicy seems, after all, to respond to a question that cannot be evaded. At some point during reflection, even those giving attention to concrete cases of suffering will ask how an all-loving Creator can be reconciled with the world as it is, and even if we are reminded of how religious words are used, the question tends to return. To me, it seems that anti-theodicy is best understood not as a position but as a continual practice – Wittgenstein would say a type of therapy – that will have to start over again each time we are led outside the bounds of words. As Pihlström notes, theodicy is less a position held by certain philosophers and more a tendency that each one of us has. Consequently, the relationship between theodicy and anti-theodicy starts to take on the form of an inner dialectic.

The Ethical Alternative

There is a need to turn away from the purely theoretical perspective and to make ethical considerations in relation to the sufferer. But how can this be a response to the problem of evil? In Section 2, I sketched out how Levinas's phenomenological analysis of pain reveals some of the essential structures of evil: it occurs to consciousness as being in opposition to consciousness itself; it is positioned as the "not" that resists integration into experience and meaning. The evils of suffering are meaningless, useless, for nothing. Despite this, evil is never without contours: it is never general and neutral, but always concrete and determined (Levinas 1998: 176). Even if evil is concrete and meaningless, Levinas does not deny that there are ways of imposing meaning on suffering, either in the hope of later progress, via an explanation of its biological or social functions, or in order to come to see suffering in other ways, as a means to an end. Certainly, religious hopes of eschatological compensation belong to this thinking, which, Levinas admits, finds legitimacy in the Bible. These are all variants of theodicy, which Levinas believes has molded the entire European mind-set in one way or another. Accordingly, its power cannot be under-estimated (Levinas 2006: 81–83).

Moreover, Levinas also claims that these various ways of imposing sense on suffering have become implausible during the twentieth century. This implausibility can be summed up in one phrase: the Holocaust, here taken as the very symbol of all atrocities and genocides that have taken place. The Holocaust is also a matter of special personal importance to Levinas himself, as a Jew who lost his family in the concentration camps. The point, as I take it, is not that the Holocaust brought out another quality of evil, but that the magnitude of it made it impossible to ignore the essential uselessness and meaninglessness of evil – as if the original sting of evil already manifest in pain became undeniably present on a grand scale. Levinas does not so much argue for the breakdown of theodicy; he simply claims that theodicy is completely out of touch with the phenomenon of evil: "The disproportion between suffering and every theodicy was shown at Auschwitz with a glaring, obvious clarity" (Levinas 2006: 84). Auschwitz, then, marks the end of theodicy. The industrial killing of Jews without any reference to guilt or sins makes theodicy not only unwarranted, but theodicy also reveals itself as utterly immoral. This immorality needs some clarification, though. For Levinas (2006: 52), the immoral character does not stem from imposing ill-founded sense on the suffering one undergoes oneself, but from imposing this sort of sense-making on others. He asks:

> But does not this end of theodicy, which imposes itself in the face of this century's inordinate trials, at the same time and in a more general way reveal the unjustifiable character of suffering in the other, the outrage it would be for me to justify my neighbor's suffering? ... [T]he justification of the neighbor's pain is certainly the source of all immorality. (Levinas 2006: 85)

If theodicy is essentially justifying my neighbor's suffering, then it is radical evil: it displays the giving of priority to myself and my meaningful world, and this includes my disregard for the real suffering of others.

In Levinas's work, the meaninglessness of the suffering of others is not the end of the story. He also provides alternative routes to theodicy in the form of considering the moral response to suffering (Levinas 2006: 80). Levinas points out that while suffering intense pain is characterized by helplessness, abandonment, and solitude – a state in which one is closed in on oneself – it also entails a "half opening." From the sufferer's point of view, this half opening comes to expression in cries for help. Seen from the perspective of those who are solicited, the meaninglessness suffering of others starts to take on meaning – more precisely, ethical meaning – as they find themselves called on, responsible, and even expected to suffer because of the suffering of others. To be exposed to a call from the sufferer is, Levinas holds, the beginning of all signification. But Levinas also speaks of a more specific, religious response to evil – and particularly the evils of the Holocaust. The question that has been asked repeatedly since the Holocaust is: where was God during those atrocities? To Levinas, there is no possible defense of God at this point; God was silent. But, nevertheless, God should not be renounced as that would be to grant the Devil right and to let National Socialism finish the message of the Bible. Since the message of the Bible in Levinas's reading is an ethical one, religion and ethics must converge. It is only thus that faith can survive evil and God's absence, giving rise to a faith beyond theodicy:

> Must not humanity now, in a faith more difficult than before, in a faith without theodicy, continue to live out sacred history; in a history that now demands even more from the resources of the *I* in each one of us, and from its suffering inspired by the suffering of the other, from its compassion which is a non-useless suffering (or love), which is no longer suffering "for nothing," and immediately has meaning? (Levinas 2006: 86)

It is from this ethical-religious perspective alone that Levinas finds a way out of the dichotomy of theodicy or meaninglessness: in taking on responsibility and non-indifference to the other, there is a half opening toward the meaning of evil.

The Cross

Levinas' ethical-religious outlook certainly resonates with Jewish thinking, but does not leave much room for the classic theistic God above and beyond our world. There is also a distinctive Christian response to the problem of evil with a clear anti-theodicist twist, as advocated by theologians such as Dietrich Bonhoeffer, Jon Sobrino, and Jürgen Moltmann. Taking as its point of departure the conviction that theodicy is an implausible response to evil, such accounts turn toward the crucifixion of Christ. Admittedly, the cross has played a part in the Christian tradition of theodicy and has, at times, been taken up too hastily as part of a divine redemptive plan and therefore lifted into the realm of abstract solutions. By downplaying the scandal of the failing and abandoned Son, there is a danger of latching on merely to the victory of the cross, a tendency that can be traced in the New Testament (Sobrino 1978: 184–190). But what if the cross does not so much offer a solution to the problem of evil as confront us with a new way of approaching the topic?

It is certain that the cross does not reveal the all-powerful God, since his only son dies a lonely and shameful death, without aid or rescue from above. Accordingly, Luther speaks of how God's might is hidden under weakness. In more recent times, Dietrich Bonhoeffer has contended that this absence of power is exactly what the cross invites us to contemplate. As he wrote in one of his letters from prison during World War II, "Christ helps us, not by virtue of his omnipotence, but by virtue of his weakness and suffering" (Bonhoeffer 2017: 134). The starting point for such an understanding of the cross in response to the problem of suffering does not just admit the bankruptcy of theodicy; it also embraces a sort of atheistic conclusion: there is an experience of being godforsaken in suffering, even for the Son of God. With Jesus's words on the cross, "My God, my God, why have you forsaken me?" (Mk. 15:34; Mt. 27:46; Psalm 22:2), a gap within divinity opens up, as Jürgen Moltmann has emphasized. This gap is between God the Father, grieving for his dying son, and the Son himself, completely abandoned by everyone – his father included (Moltmann 1974: 154).

To many Jewish thinkers, Levinas among them, the Holocaust does not offer any revelation regarding God – no sense of a special presence through suffering. Indeed, it makes God's absence manifest. There is a much-quoted passage in *Night*, Elie Wiesel's memoirs from Auschwitz, that picks up on the absence of God. After a failed sabotage attempt, two men and a young boy are hanged at the camp. All the prisoners are forced to watch the execution, and the boy struggles in the gallows for a very long time. Wiesel hears someone behind him asking where the supposedly merciful God is now. This idea is repeated again a little later: "Behind me, I heard the same man asking: 'For God's sake, where is God?' And from within me, I heard a voice answer: 'Where is He? This is where – hanging here from this gallows'" (Wiesel 2006: 65). The most likely interpretation of this passage, I assume, is that God dies in the gallows with the boy; a "death of God" in a Nietzschean sense, which makes it impossible for faith to be maintained. There is another possibility, however, as explained by Moltmann: in this reading, a weak God is present – not one that offers escapes and miraculous solutions but one that is there, nonetheless. By means of the cross, Christ is partaking in the senseless human agony that unfolds.

As Moltmann has it, the point of God becoming human and undergoing the trial of the cross is not to assure us of the justification of evil from the standpoint of an omnipotent and omniscient God; instead, on the cross God becomes completely one with suffering humanity. But if identification and solidarity are the central messages of the cross, then a radical revision of theistic and metaphysical depictions of God is required. The conception of God as absolutely enhanced beyond human affections and feelings is a Greek understanding that was taken up by the Church Fathers (Moltmann 1974: 277–280).

However, if the cross reveals who God is – one who suffers a physical death in complete isolation – then the notion of the Greek-influenced impassable God simply does not fit. Commenting on Wiesel's silent reply that God is hanging in the gallows, Moltmann (1974: 283) suggests that the God in the gallows is realized in Christ on the cross: "Any other answer would be blasphemy. There cannot be any other Christian answer to the question of this torment. To speak here of a God who could not suffer would make God a demon. To speak here of an absolute God would make God an annihilating nothingness." The idea is that if God is love, then He must be vulnerable to caring and feeling concerned for His creatures. Such vulnerability is not a lack, as the Greeks thought; on the contrary, it provides the conditions for love – the very love at the base of the relationship between the Father and the Son. Moltmann argues that it is only against such background that we can see the full drama of the cross: a drama unfolding between the Father and Son, through the Holy Spirit, between Creator and creation. Again, this interpretation offers no solution or theodicy, but merely a perspective through which lived, meaningless suffering can gain orientation and a sense of divine acknowledgment. God is there, hanging on the cross; thus, human suffering is taken into the Godhead itself.

The Dynamics between Theodicy and Anti-Theodicy

Returning to the Book of Job, the dialogue between Job and his friends appears as a broken dialogue, with the parties speaking past one another. As Job views it, the friends are doing nothing to recognize his pain. But there is no doubt that they respond. Their justifications and explanations appear to Job as their excuses, as if they are turning the attention away from the uncomfortable presence of his suffering and the difficulty of understanding God's role in it. Why? Perhaps they are attempting to avoid not just the troublesome facts that Job represents but also what these facts reveal about themselves: that the harsh reality outruns the limits of their comprehension, and that we are all potentially exposed to suffering evils for no apparent reason. If so, their attitudes can be said to be "skeptical," in Stanley Cavell's sense of evading what our words and our reality mean. Whether expressed as doubt or certainty, Cavell (1979: 109) believes that the skeptic expresses the wish to deny the human condition. And strangely, precisely such a skeptic reaction is all too human: "Nothing is more human than the wish to deny one's humanity, or to assert it at the expense of others." According to such an interpretation, the friends' skepticism deflects attention away from themselves, enabling them to prevent self-exposure to what Cora Diamond (2008: 45–46) calls "the difficulty of reality": a reality that is undeniably present, but is too hard and painful to take in.

One might ask, however, if Job's friends and theodicy in general give voice to nothing but avoidance and deflection. The problem repeats itself, for by leaning on this common reading of the friends, one seems to be guilty of the same charge: avoiding their voice and deflecting their claims. After all, it has been suggested that what they provide are the resources that can offer Job a new orientation – resources perhaps meant to facilitate a more consoling narrative of his shattered life (Newsom 2009: 125). Attempting to save the traditional conception of God from the problem of evil is not, at least not necessarily, an escape from the issue at hand. What I am suggesting is that a critique of theodicy is, indeed, necessary, but one should acknowledge, none-theless, that theodicy grows out of a natural reaction. As long as there is evil, people will go on asking themselves "Why? Why me? How could God allow this to happen?" Phillips argues that such questions, when raised by a sufferer, are not seeking any response at all – and particularly not an explanation in the form of a super-explanation. Nevertheless, the drive to seek out answers belongs to the thinking animals that we are, hence philosophical and theological responses remain to be made, if not necessarily arguments and abstract systems. Indeed, theodicy enables us to respond to those questions intellectually. Even though moral attentiveness is called for, such moral attentiveness does not mean that the intellectual challenge of evil simply vanishes, as Hick (2010: 9) argues. It is even possible to suggest that the questions theodicy responds to are rooted in the phenomenon of pain itself, ripping us out of metaphysical heedlessness and exposing us to the question of "Why?" If, at times, anti-theodicists take too easily such a truth within theodicy, then they are failing to acknowledge their interlocutors, which is ironic, given that acknowledgment of the other is one of anti-theodicy's prime concerns.

In Cavell's view, there is a dialectic between the skeptical and the anti-skeptical impulse, which plays itself out within us as a dialectic between internal voices. Thus, as the voice of theodicy aims at justification, the voice of anti-theodicy will point out its emptiness and give it up all together. Both voices are inextricably connected in the search for explanations for the problem of evil, either affirming or denying it. What is needed to get out of this locked situation is perhaps to "think more and otherwise," to repeat Ricoeur's phrase: beyond knowledge and explanation. Such thinking requires not more knowledge or reason, but something else, such as acknowledgment. Acknowledgment, Cavell has argued, is not a dismissal of knowledge but a way to embrace knowledge as rooted in a more primordial type of attention and response, which goes beyond theoretical knowledge – such as when we comfort another in pain. Importantly, acknowledgment also entails revealing something negative about the self: recognizing the tendency to avoid our acknowledgment of others, ourselves, and God (Cavell 1976: 256–264).

If theodicy responds to the right questions, but fails in its answers, then anti-theodicy is wrong in rejecting theodicy's impulse to respond but right in questioning the mode of theodicy's typical answers. They are both skeptic and yet they both entail some truth. Anti-theodicy involves leading that response back to the acknowledgment of a difficult reality: that evil is present in the suffering of others and myself, and that God must be acknowledged beyond an image of metaphysical omnipotence. Still, to search for ethical and intellectual responses to evil is not meaningless or inherently perverse in itself, but natural. However, aiming for a total solution is conceptually problematic and, furthermore, pulls us in a dangerous direction: toward avoidance and denial. Perhaps we must conclude that an attempt to think through the problem of evil becomes an infinite philosophical and theological task, in which the constant new beginning is generated with each encounter with evil. Cavell (1988: 5) concludes aptly here that the task of philosophy is one of neither affirming nor refuting skepticism; instead, the task is to "preserve it, as though the philosophical profit of the argument would be to show not how it might end but why it must begin and why it must have no end, at least none within philosophy, or what we think of as philosophy."

4 God's Revelation: Images of God

The Book of Job has been taken as a tragedy, in which the hero keeps to an unverifiable faith and yet suffers pain beyond any explanation (Ricoeur 1967: 321–323). It has also been interpreted as a comedy, either due to the restoration at the end or, more speculatively, because of Job's moral victory over God (Tennessen 1973: 9). Still, most readers regard the Book of Job as neither a tragedy nor a comedy, seeing it instead as a book of edifying virtues or, conversely, as a book of protest. The approach one takes depends on one's reply to the question of who Job is and who Job's God is. Of course, this question about God is not just one among others but is perhaps the most central question of the book – and of theology and the philosophy of religion in general. Where the text is concerned, the lack of a simple and widely accepted answer to this question can be seen as due partly to the openness and complexity of Job's story, as well as to the ever-changing contexts in which the meaning of the text is considered. In a religious text like the Book of Job, God is all over the place, playing a significant role in the prologue, being hotly discussed in the dialogue, and restoring Job in the epilogue. Nevertheless, it is God's own self-revelation that must be given most weight in relation to discerning God's identity, and so we must turn to the theophany, where God addresses Job directly.

The Theophany from the Whirlwind

"Then the LORD answered Job out of the whirlwind ... 'Where were you when I laid the foundation of the world?'" (Job 38:1, 4). These words, taken from the opening of the theophany, are perhaps the most famous in the Book of Job. In fact, the theophany consists of not one, but two speeches. The first gives a sweeping glance over creation (Job 38–39), while the second focuses on the monsters Behemoth and Leviathan (Job 40:6–41). The two speeches are separated by a short intermezzo, in which Job replies briefly (Job 40:3–5), and the section is rounded off with Job repenting in dust and ashes (Job 42:1–5). As one can tell already from this brief exposition, it is no surprise that commentators have asked whether God really replies to Job's appeals. On one hand, there is no mention of Job's suffering here; what is elicited, rather, is an inhuman world. On the other hand, however, one cannot take lightly the fact that God does respond to Job and address him, which is exactly what Job has longed for. Indeed, in the biblical universe, meeting or seeing God is a very rare honor; in most cases, it is forbidden and even dangerous to draw near to God. Moses, for instance, is allowed only to see the back of God as he passes (Ex. 33:23). Moreover, God singles out Job as a "You," just as Job has previously addressed God directly, and thus a personal, dialogical relation is established between them, even if it is asymmetrical.

In the first speech, God brings Job along on a cosmic tour, as it were, from heavenly phenomena to the animal world. The cosmic perspective is already announced with the theme of the foundation of the Earth, where God presents Himself as the Creator and upholder of the universe. God not only lays the foundation below us; He is also the maker of the stars above us, clouds and lightning, darkness and light. God is the one that controls meteorological phenomena such as snow and rain, ice and frost (Job 38:19–38). Closing in on the Earth, God proceeds to account for the animal world. In a long poetic passage, He picks out a series of examples, underlining how the animals are under His constant providence: He provides prey for the lion and the raven, and keeps time for the birth of mountain goats and deer. He offers a place for the wild ass and is the master of the wild ox. Even the ostrich, which, out of oblivion or stupidity, can crush its own eggs, is made so by God, just like the fearless, impressive wild horse and the eagle (Job 38:39–39:30). This over-whelming bombardment of snapshots from the created universe proves enough to strike the otherwise talkative Job dumb: "See, I am a small account; what shall I answer you? I lay my hand on my mouth" (Job 40:4).

But God is not finished. His second speech moves on to more uncanny territory: that of monsters. This is not the first time that monsters are mentioned in the book – in fact, of all the biblical books, this is one of the most densely populated with monster figures. Job mentions Leviathan, Rahab, and the serpent, all images borrowed from the pantheon known to the ancient Near East (Job 3:8, 26:12–13). In God's speech, the monsters return with full force and are given lengthy accounts about their beauty and danger. First, there is Behemoth, who appears like a giant hippopotamus and whose strength, fear-lessness, and massive constitution are underlined. The danger that this monster suggests can be matched only by God's sword but, interestingly, it is also made clear that the creature is God's creation (Job 49:15–23). Proceeding to Leviathan, God presents an aquatic monster, one that is even more threatening and sublime. Leviathan looks somewhat like giant crocodile, shielded with impenetrable skin and teeth, and moving around the sea like gigantic whale, while breathing fire like a dragon. Rhetorically, God asks Job: "Can you draw out Leviathan with a fish hook, or press down its tongue with a cord?" (Job 41:1). Thus God underlines the smallness and powerlessness of Job compared to this beast. But it is not just Job who is no match for Leviathan, for there is no one – not even the gods – who can confront it and be safe, except God.

It is noteworthy that the speeches taken together deal undoubtedly with the matter of creation, but in reverse order, as it were. Whereas the story of the creation in six days, as accounted for in Genesis, starts with chaotic water and wasteland, and moves on to the development of well-ordered creation, God's speeches here run the other way. Starting with the relatively stable order of the cosmos, Heaven, and meteorology, the monologue moves on to wild animals, ending up with a threatening sea monster that challenges God's order (Doak 2015: 275). Perhaps this suggests both the non-ending enterprise of creation and the presence of chaos. Whatever it signifies, it is more than enough for Job. He has not only seen creation in its magnificence and dread, gaining sublime insight; he has also, more importantly, seen God: "Therefore I have uttered what I did not understand, things too wonderful for me, which I did not know . . . I had heard of you by the hearing of the ear, but no eyes have seen you; therefore I despise myself, and repent in dust and ashes" (Job 42:3, 5–6). The latter clause is difficult to interpret; it is far from clear that Job despises himself, although he does seem to repent somehow. Indeed, this matter has troubled scholars such as Tilley (2000: 96–102), who explores no fewer than six renderings of the relevant words, along with their different implications.

In any case, Job has seen something and has changed – that much is clear. Why does he change, though? Is it due to God's display of brute power? Is it as if, as Terry Eagleton (2010: 142) puts it, God more or less asks Job to go to Hell? Does God frighten Job into silence? Or does God let Job see something that gives him new confidence in his God?

1 The Violent God

It is not hard to find support for the notion of a violent God in the speeches. In such a reading, the power that He displays over His creation seems indifferent to weak and needy humans. In fact, God says nothing about Job's suffering, giving no explanations to him and saying nothing to prove Job right – He does not even express sympathy (Morriston 1996: 341). Instead, God focuses on meteorology, zoology, and mythology. If one pays attention to the animals that God chooses to present, it is striking that they are all wild; that is, untamed by cultivation and human order, hence presenting the outland, the waste, the uninhabitable (Newsome 2009: 245). The threats of the wild ox and the fearlessness of a war horse signify powers beyond human control. The foolishness and cruelty of the ostrich, which crushes its own eggs, is hardly meant to underline God's loving care. Arguably, the lion, who needs prey, which God provides, and the eagle, which He lets feed on slain human corpses (letting their "young ones suck up blood"; Job 39:30) do so even less. They seem, rather, to present a version of creation that works independently of any moral law – one in which untamed cruelty, stupidity, and blind forces are at work.

Such a view is perhaps not foreign to modern naturalistic outlooks, where life is seen as unfolding in a universe according to the universe's own impersonal laws. However, by means of repeated rhetorical questions to Job, God is making His point univocally clear: this creation is His personal doing. Of course, things do not get better in the accounts of the monsters, the strength of which cannot be matched by anyone except God. In contrast to the creation depicted in Genesis, it is not at all certain here that human beings are the crowning glory of this creation. As God says, Behemoth is made, just as Job is, indeed, Behemoth "is the first of the great acts of God" (Job 40:19). What kind of God is this? Herman Tennessen's (1973: 10) answer reads: "He represents a familiar biological and social milieu: the blind forces of nature, completely indifferent to the human need for order and meaning and justice ... : the unpredictable visitation by disease and death, the transitoriness of fame, the treason for friends and kin."

Perhaps, then, the speeches make manifest something that Job has known since the onset of his suffering: the Law, which comprises the moral, cultic, and juridical regulations entailed in the covenant, does not apply to this God. As Job suspects, there is no correspondence between sin and his pain, and, further, righteousness and reward. As it seems, God's Law has very limited application in this world. In his speculative and fascinating book, Philippe Nemo does not hesitate to identify God with evil, although he will also say that God eventually turns good. Job's God remains the "Wholly Other": an evil radically separated from all that we take as constituting the world, i.e., the ways in which we habituate ourselves with techniques and orders to preserve the good. Nemo will not buy into Tennessen's God of blind natural forces, however, because then suffering would contain no religious or personal importance to Job, which it certainly does. Evil hits him personally from another You, who afflicts Job in a capricious manner. Or, even worse, as Nemo (1998: 105) writes: "The Caprice is not pure contingency, it takes *interest* in me, and, being interested, it *desires* my suffering." In being aimed at by the divine You, Nemo argues, Job is making a horrible discovery about God. The excess of this evil has no earthly explanation and it strikes independently of any law. The Law always comes too late in the attempt to restrain and control disorder. This is why the friends' appeal to the Law makes no sense to Job, for Job's God does not correspond with the Law at all, but breaks through its jurisdiction (Nemo 1998: 90–91).

Nemo's point is not so much to portray a violent God as to describe the excessive otherness of evil as it occurs to Job – the way that evil breaks Job off from the world and puts him in immediate relation to God. This is very different from Nehama Verbin's (2010: 139) reading, which takes Job's God as a moral agent, but an agent that, nonetheless, falls short of moral standards. Verbin argues that the biblical narrator not only paints Job's misfortunes in stark colors, but also explicitly identifies God as responsible for the misfortunes that occur. Job has no problem with tracing back his malady to God: "Have pity on me, have pity on me, O you my friends, for the hand of God has touched me!" (Job 19:21). But there is more, for Job is not only suffering, Verbin argues, but undergoing divine abuse. "Abuse involves more than suffering," she explains, "[i]t involves an agent who is morally responsible for the infliction of suffering, which is viewed as an injustice; it carries an address and words of disapprobation with it. It is suffering stamped with the fingerprints of an abuser" (Verbin 2010: xii). It makes no difference whether God Himself inflicts harm or lets Satan perform it because the moral responsibility is God's anyway.

Admittedly, God singles Job out among all the entities in the universe, but such an act of recognition is not favorable in this case because the recognition comes through violent acts. According to Verbin, however, it is not just physical attacks that are at stake; God is also transgressing all conceptions of justice, and He insults Job's sense of self-worth. The attack on justice gives rise to what Verbin calls "moral hatred," which is directed at the violation of morality. The attack on Job's self-worth creates resentment, as seen in Job's protesting anger against God's attempt to devalue him (Verbin 2010: 31–32). The theophany does not alter any of this impression in Verbin's reading, as it merely fleshes out the lack of morality in the natural world and the social world alike. Thus, the divine speeches are nothing but a display of brute power. What Job comes to realize, in Verbin's understanding, is that, despite God's overpowering might, Job can preserve his own self-worth because he is superior to God in one important respect: morality. The idea of Job's superiority to God was first proposed by C. G. Jung (2011: 21, 43), who argues that God is less than human in his lack of self-reflection. For Verbin, Job discovers God's lack of power over his moral judgment on one hand, and the lack of God's own proper morality on the other.

Dorothee Soelle takes up this idea that Job is "stronger than God" – not in might, of course, but in his capacity to reject God as a tyrant. She interprets Job via the background of a long theological tradition that she finds strangely sadomasochistic. First, this tradition is masochistic on the part of the believers, who think that suffering is the means to bring them closer to God, leading them to submit themselves to suffering without question. Second, it is sadistic, with respect to the image of God, depicted as inflicting pain and eternal punishment above our heads – a depiction she finds particularly prominent in the Reformation era, and most explicitly in Calvin (Soelle 1975: 22–24). When it comes to the Book of Job, Soelle finds nothing new or exceptional about a tyrant who puts His servants through an ordeal, since this motif is widespread in myths and folktales. Whereas the hero is usually tested via challenging tasks that must be overcome, no such challenge is at stake in the Book of Job. God is not testing skills, but simply hands Job over to pain and suffering. In God's own speeches, as we have seen, God highlights his power and, by implication, belittles Job. In this way, the revealed God repeats the sadistic structure: He demands Job's submission to Him and His powers, regardless of any justice. Is this really the same God that dominates the biblical account elsewhere: the God that takes the side of the victims, leads the people of Israel out of Egypt, and speaks through the prophet against misuse of power? Not according to Soelle: "This God is a nature demon, who bears no relation to the God of Exodus and of the prophets" (Soelle 1975: 117). Job's exceptional rejection of God, then, is matched by the exceptional depiction of his God.

It appears that Verbin and Soelle's analyses are based on a modern conception of morality, in which human justice and rights are laid down as the first principles through which the qualities of God are assessed. In this respect, they resemble modern theodicists, even if their goal is not to defend God but to criticize damaging pictures of Him. It is necessary to keep in mind the many ways in which religion can be misused – for power struggles, for reinforcing sexism or racism, or for other ideological means. Such decided premises, however, tend to produce rather one-sided depictions of Job's God. Given the complexity and multiplicity of the Book of Job, it is worth asking if such understandings of the Joban God are too narrow.

2 The Weak God

In presenting a transitional position between the violent God and the weak God, René Girard has provided a fascinating, yet speculative reading. He concurs that Job is subject to intolerable violence, but believes that the violence is human rather than divine. Girard employs his general theory of how violence evolves according to mutual imitation, how violence produces societal crisis, and finally leads to the search for scapegoats. In the present reading, Job is picked out as society's more or less arbitrary victim. The friends are just representatives of society inflicting him with all kinds of evils, even though Job is innocent. They produce mythologies designed to justify the unjust lynching of the scapegoat. The members of society know secretly that if they can channel all the potential violence into one victim, the steam is let out, and they will regain a general state of peace and stability (Girard 1987: 69). The only problem is that Job will not give in to such myths; he keeps on protesting his innocence. Indeed, he appeals to another God beyond those myths: a witness that will argue his case in Heaven or even, ultimately, take his side (Job 16:19, 19:25–27). "Deprived of all human support," Girard (1987: 139) writes, "the victim turns to God; he embraces the concept of a God of victims. He does not permit his persecutors to monopolize the idea of God."

The most profitable upshot of Girard's reading is his image of God as being unfailingly on the victim's side. Since Auschwitz, however, the problems inherent with such a conviction have become particularly pressing, especially among Jews. Was God silent during the massacre of His people? Was He really on the victims' side? Or did He just let it happen? Jewish philosopher Hans Jonas has offered an important reflection on this topic, arguing that the problem is not new, but is already reverberating in the Book of Job. However, for Jonas, the problem came to the fore with a new intensity and in a more paradoxical fashion in the twentieth century: election, once at the heart of the covenant between God and His people, was turned upside down into a monstrous process, in which this people was elected for death camps. Moreover, God let this happen (Jonas 1987: 3). Note, however, that Jonas holds that God did not permit this out of cruelty. Jonas does not even entertain the notion of a tyrannical God, as discussed by Soelle and others; rather, Jonas's key question is: "Why did God not intervene?" The question is enigmatic only if one presupposes that God is fundamentally good. Jonas has little patience with the theistic God that is safely distinct from the world, being immutable, impassable, and eternal. He sees the Creator as not being above creation at all; instead, He gave literally all He had in creating the world. In this reading, God has poured Himself out into His own creation, which implies that He remains dependent on the world's development over time, including its inherent dangers and risks. As such, God took a risk in creating free and responsible human beings.

When Jonas raises the problem of evil, he begins with the matter of how the evil in the world can be reconciled with an omnipotent and wholly good God. One way to reach a conclusion and keep these premises unaltered, he contends, is by sacrificing God's intelligibility. A good God creating a world with so much evil is simply beyond any comprehension. Even if there is a long tradition of speaking about the hidden God, Jonas finds such a conception un-Jewish, since the entire teaching of the Torah rests on the notion that it is possible to understand God. As already noted, though, goodness cannot be removed without losing the idea of God. If He will not sacrifice intelligibility and goodness, what about omnipotence? In line with Phillips and others, Jonas is highly skeptical of this traditional term. First, he argues logically, the concept of omnipotence is self-contradictory. If one imagines an absolutely unrestricted power, there can be absolutely no obstacles that limit it. But, without any other opposing the omnipotent entity, Jonas infers, there is nothing to exercise power over, and so the whole notion becomes empty. Since power is relational, then, omnipotence in such an absolute sense is self-defeating (Jonas 1987: 8).

In a more theological register, Jonas argues that renouncing omnipotence will lead to a new consideration of the relationship between God's goodness and evil. He writes that,

> his goodness must be compatible with the existence of evil, and
> this it is only if he is not *all* powerful. Only then can we uphold
> that he is intelligible and good, and there is yet evil in the world.
> And since we have found the concept of omnipotence to be
> dubious anyway, it is this that has to give way. (Jonas 1987: 10)

The God that Jonas has in mind is still the Creator of the universe, but He is one that has created by restricting Himself and pouring all His resources out into creation. Thus, God was silent during Auschwitz not because He was standing secretly behind the events or because He chose not to intervene; having given His all, there was simply no more that God could do. In short, God has handed history over to humanity. This is, indeed, an attempted answer to Job's question, an answer that has both similarities and dissimilarities with the solution that the book proposes. Alluding to the theophany, Jonas (1987: 13) writes that the Book of Job "invoked the plenitude of God's power; mine, his chosen avoidance of it. And yet, strange to say, both are in praise."

Jonas's Jewish approach has some very clear affinities with Christian approaches to evil. As seen in the previous section, Moltmann makes a comparable appeal to divine weakness, and Eberhard Jüngel (2003: 160) also affirms Jonas's account, although both theologians add the important qualification that divine weakness and human evil find their proper expression on the cross. Despite all this, the weak and suffering God, who gives all He has in caring for creation, still seems a far cry from the God who speaks to Job. Jonas may read the Book of Job as expressing the "plenitude of God's power," but is this necessarily so?

Biblical scholar André LaCocque has found the Joban God to be a weak God, based on an interpretation of the theophany, which is precisely where the proponents of the "violent God" seem to find their best textual support. Since God elaborates on His creation here, it is critical to examine how this creation is depicted. LaCocque's view turns around the most common reading of the theophany, in which God is simply displaying the sublime things that He has the power to make. According to LaCocque's (1996: 139) reading, the world God presents to Job is not a closed order governed by retributive justice but a dynamic whole, containing both good and evil, light and darkness, lawfulness and lawlessness – a world that demands God's constant personal care and agency. More precisely, creation brings the cosmos out of formless and destructive chaos: "The cosmic laws in the hands of God continuously prevent the universe from sinking back into chaos. The truth of the matter is that there is lawlessness in the creation . . . There is wickedness, *but* it is not unbounded" (LaCocque 2007: 85).

As in the first creation story, God creates from chaotic or desolate material: "the earth was a formless void and darkness covered the face of the deep" (Gen. 1:2). In God's speech, the emphasis is laid on measurement, boundaries, and active limitation. Such notions are prevalent when God speaks of the sea, which is associated with the formless, dissolving, and chaotic forces that threaten order (Job 38:8–11). For reasons that remain unexplained in the Book of Job, powers exist that God needs to hold in check continuously: "Or who shut in the sea with doors when it burst out from the womb? – when I . . . prescribed the bounds for it, and set bars and doors and said, 'This far shall you come, and no further, and here shall your proud waves be stopped?'" (Job 39: 8–11). Notably, LaCocque does not shy away from the fact that there is more than a hint of absurdity in this creation: God lets the rain fall everywhere – even in the desert, where it is to no avail; He brings forth wild animals, which arouse fear in human beings. This impression of absurdity is enhanced further as God turns to the monsters of Behemoth and Leviathan. For LaCocque, all these examples bring attention to the dark side of creation, which Job himself has experienced and to which God is far from indifferent. With providence and care, God works constantly to restrain the chaos of evil. The present world as it stands is not safe from evil, according to the biblical depiction; in Jon Levenson's (1988: 48) words, the Bible depicts the world "*before* rather than *after* the triumph of God."

Why does God not address Job's pain, then, if He cares for this created man? The answer is that perhaps God does address it indirectly, if not directly. The theophany could be interpreted as showing God's care for His creation: His provision of shelter and food for the wild animals, His choice to provide water, and so on. Eleonore Stump has argued at length that, far from being a demonstration of indifferent power, the theophany displays God's unfailing relationship and paternal care for His creatures – and, consequently, for Job. In her interpretation, the fact that God engages in a face-to-face dialogue with Job is the most important event: such a personal experience has the power to change Job's view of what he considered previously to be an abusing God (Stump 2012: 186–192). LaCocque thinks along the same lines but adds a further twist to the reading. The major parts of God's speeches are made up of questions to Job, as if God is now challenging Job's own questions and thereby turning Job's view around. The perspective is no longer Job's – i.e., the perspective of the individual sufferer toward a meaningless universe; instead, it turns toward the immensity of the universe and then back to Job, who has a place in it, but is only a small part of it. As a result, Job comes to recognize that his suffering belongs to the dark side that God continually opposes. Although the view of an omnipotent God has to give way in LaCocque's reading, this weaker God is still a caring God and, most important of all, He is – echoing Girard – on Job's side. LaCocque (2007: 94) sums up the implications of this God of the theophany by stating that: "God the Creator has chosen to manifest power through weakness, that is, through shedding off abscondence and becoming involved in a two-way communication with his creature."

I do see such a reading as plausible and, indeed, preferable to that of the violent God. But it also gives rise to some questions. The first is an exegetical one: can an unbiased reading of the book, particularly where God's portrayed in the theophany as concerned, support the notion of such a weak but caring God? Discussing the wild animals in the first speech, Wesley Morriston (1996: 349) does "not find . . . the slightest intimation of the sort of providential care that would justify Job in expecting God to do anything for him." Any support of LaCocque's view will take some broader contextualizing in the biblical and theological landscape – which he has, indeed, provided elsewhere. Theologically speaking, it is true that a weak God that identifies with human suffering has been proposed by many twentieth-century philosophers and theologians, including Bonhoeffer, Moltmann, Jüngel, Jonas, and Vattimo. To some, however, such as Muslim author Navid Kermani, an emphasis on weakness robs us of trust in God's capacity and power to help. Citing Karl Rahner, Kermani writes: "when I am trying to get out of my dirt, chaos and despair, what good does it do me to know that God – crudely put – feels just as rotten?" (Kermani 2011: 99). But then, the ultimate question is whether or not the alternative is tenable any longer.

Job's Insight

Undoubtedly, the theophany provokes a change in Job. At first glance, this change seems to give support to the latter reading, where Job has found a God – sublime, no doubt, but still caring enough for Job to find his way back to Him. Indeed, why would Job retract his words and repent, if he still believed that God was a tyrant who abused him or a capricious nature demon? There are possible ways to make sense of this. Tennessen suggests that what Job discovers is that, despite God's quantitative greatness, He is qualitatively small, intellectually and morally speaking. This sheds a merciless light on Job's final withdrawal: "By capitulating in this manner, he inflicts the worst conceivable of indignities on the tyrant, Jehovah: that his opponent is not even worthy of a battle" (Tennessen 1973: 9).

All the readings that find God tyrannical have problems in coming to terms with the end of the drama – not so much the change, but the fact that Job dies "old and full of days" (Job 42:17). This outcome is either discarded or, as in Tennessen's work, taken as fraudulent. Another often unthematized premise for opting for a violent God is that Job's God remains unaltered and identical throughout the text. Clearly, Job identifies God as the one who hurts him, and this seems to correspond neatly with a God that creates a universe indifferent to human well-being. But the text suggests strongly that Job changes his view, especially in the two confessions toward the end (Job 40:3–5, 42:1–6). As Martin Buber (1969) has argued, the story of Job offers a succession of different conceptions of God – he finds no fewer than four such conceptions at work. If we take this approach, then it is possible to assert that Job gradually discovers that he was wrong initially; not about his pain, of course, but about the author of his pain. God did not desire to make him His target. What the reading of the weak God suggests is that Job learns that his suffering is part of the dimension of reality that God opposes. Behind the pain, then, is what we might call Satan, or any mythical figure used to express the undeniable and inexplicable presence of evils in the world. As LaCocque (2007: 94) puts it: "His repentance is an acknowledgement not of legal culpability in the eyes of others, but of having believed in a faulty theological construct . . . He realizes that he was never God's target, but, in a still unaccomplished creation, he was unwittingly swept into the whirlwind of its dark side."

And yet does the appeal to a weak God not fly in the face of the biblical notion of the almighty God? In a sense, it does, if might is interpreted according to the abstract metaphysical concept of unrestricted omnipotence. But, then again, such an interpretation hardly squares with the biblical use of "almighty," either. Its linguistic home is not that of metaphysics; rather, it belongs to a religious or, perhaps more aptly, liturgical context: that of doxology or cultic praise (Hygen 1974: 133–134). In praise, as in poetry, words are stretched and opened up to a wider horizon of sense, without cutting their anchorage in ordinary use. Praise of the almighty God has its own grammar, which confines it from lending itself to abstract and universal propositions. Hence, God the almighty has powers with regard to the world; it is not said, however, that God has powers beyond any conceivable restrictions. This almighty God is demonstrated most vividly when God prevails over opposing forces or bestows His creatures with the good things of His creation.

Epilogue

Shortly, I close this Element with the brief ending with which the Book of Job concludes: its epilogue (Job 42:7–17). After having retracted his words and bowed in dust and ashes, Job is declared by God to have spoken rightly of Him, unlike his friends (Job 42:8). It is hard to tell exactly what Job retracts or, similarly, what God acknowledges as being right. If Job comes to the conviction, as I hold, that he has accused God of a suffering that God did not inflict, then it can be suggested that Job withdraws the accusations and complaints that run through the dialogue. Nevertheless, God seems to hold that there is some truth in what Job, as opposed to his friends, has said: "My wrath is kindled against you and against your two friends; for you have not spoken of me what is right, as my servant Job has" (Job 42:7). We are not told to what God is referring. Maybe it is Job's conviction that the living God cannot fit into the neat system of dogmatic and ethical views held by his friends; perhaps, as Kant would insist, God approves of Job's unflinching integrity. Whatever it might be, God restores all Job's former fortunes; indeed, "the LORD gave Job twice as much as he had before" (Job 42:10). Family and friends return to him, he receives three daughters and seven sons, and, finally, he dies "old and full of days" (Job 42:17).

A happy ending, to be sure. Are these not just the kind of platitudes, though, that we would expect from a Hollywood production? Can this be taken seriously as the book's conclusion? It seems like a total collapse, in view of the lengthy accounts about the most pressing religious and existential problems that are given, taking the reader from the depth of human suffering to the sublimity of God's revelation. "It is difficult to take this farce seriously," Girard (1987: 142) complains; Soelle (1975: 118) finds the epilogue simply "incredible and intolerable." Indeed, for Wiesel, the real offense of the book is not Job's rebellion against God, but the ending. Why would Job, having gone through all that misery, simply get down on his knees? "I prefer to think," Wiesel (1976: 233) tells us, "that the Book's true ending was lost. That Job died without having repented, without having humiliated himself; that he succumbed to his grief as an uncompromising and whole man." Verbin (2010) also offers a reading along these lines. As she puts it, in the end, there is no question of divine grace being offered to Job but, rather, we see God's attempt to bribe Job, bringing him back into the fold. The twist comes, however, when Job forgives God, and not because of God's flattery but because Job has restored his own sense of dignity. The forgiveness Verbin has in mind is not a matter of turning the heart totally toward such an unrelenting abuser, for the moral hatred of God's injustice subsists. Having restored his self-worth, however, Job can maintain a minimal, yet still active relationship with God (Verbin 2010: 140–142).

But what if the epilogue has something more to tell us? Something beyond God's flattery or the shallow happy ending? Maybe it points toward the coming world, as an enigmatic sign we cannot fully decipher. Or maybe the ending is less about God's miraculous gifts or promises and has more to do with the notion of regaining one's ordinary life after experiencing pain and suffering. If one changes the perspective, moving away from God's sudden change toward Job and the alteration that he has undergone, then one might take the conclusion to indicate that Job returns to his former view: "The LORD gave, and the LORD has taken away; blessed be the name of the LORD" (Job 1:21). There are, as Ricoeur has argued, clear tragic traits in the story, such as the clash between necessity and human freedom. Tellingly, though, Job comes eventually to find a way of embracing both necessity and freedom as elements of his fate, an interpretation in which both the good and the bad are given by God (Ricoeur 1967: 322). In a similar vein, Carol A. Newsom (2009: 258) suggests that the epilogue gestures toward a reconciliation between the sublimity of God's revelation and the possibility of life, in which Job regains his ability to live and to love.

Both Ricoeur and Newsom argue that the ending points beyond tragedy to some sense of the regaining of life as the pain is lifted. In the epilogue, we are brought back, in a strange way, to the beginning: the former life is given back to Job – his earthly goods, even his children. But, of course, it would be naïve to accept this as if nothing had happened in between, as if what returns to him is simply the same as before. For instance, Job obviously cannot get back the same children that he lost, which I take to indicate that there is a change integral to the return. It is not so much a going back, then, as a going on. The restored Job, it can be assumed, is now living with the knowledge that a terrible gap can open up any time, for evil strikes independently of law, order, and anticipation. Job's trial has broken down the sense of childlike immediacy, as Kierkegaard puts it, in which everything can be taken for granted. But the possibility of some sort of gap opening up is also an occasion for what Kierkegaard (2009: 73–74) terms "repetition": having lost everything, Job is confronted with the immediacy of God in His revelation, and then regains everything. Returning to his former life, everything is the same, but also different. The possibility of evil is never removed from the renewed life, but there is still room to welcome the gift of life: it is not taken for granted, but is a gift of regeneration.

I have spent most of the pages of this Element on different aspects of the problem of evil. At the end, I must confess that the problem is still there, unresolved; hopefully, however, the problem has been given some clearer contours. Evil is there but should not exist – and that is a paradox that is hard to bridge. Indeed, the paradox seems to be anchored in the phenomenon of evil itself. But what the epilogue of the Book of Job can be taken as suggesting is another problem that is equally inscrutable: the problem of the good. This ending provokes the question, "Why do I receive the gift of life?" This question is an exclamation of joy, and perhaps praise and gratitude. In life as we know it, it sits side by side with Job's question, "Why does evil befall me?" Perhaps both the problem of evil and the problem of goodness are mysteries to thought and existence because they entail no knowable and controllable objects; rather, they appear as two enigmatic poles, according to which we orient our entire existence.

Bibliography

Augustine. 1992. *Confessions*. Translated by Henry Chadwick. Oxford: Oxford University Press.

　2003. *City of God*. Translated by Henry Bettenson. London: Penguin Books.

　2006. "The Nature of the Good." In *Augustine: Earlier Writings*. Edited and translated by J. H. S. Burleigh. Louisville, KY: Westminster John Knox Press.

　2013. *Handbook on Faith, Hope, and Love*. Translated by Albert Outler. New York, NY: Createdspace Independent Publisher.

Barth, Karl. 1960. *Church Dogmatics: The Doctrine of Creation. Volume III. Part 3*. Translated by G. W. Bromiley and R. J. Ehrlich. Edited by G. W. Bromiley and T. F. Torrance. London: T&T Clark.

Bernstein, J. M. 2015. *Torture and Dignity: An Essay on Moral Injury*. Chicago, IL: University of Chicago Press.

Bernstein, Richard J. 2002. *Radical Evil: A Philosophical Interrogation*. Cambridge: Polity Press.

Bonhoeffer, Dietrich. 2017. *Letters and Papers from Prison*. Edited by Eberhard Bethge. Translated by J. Bowden. London: SCM Press.

Buber, Martin. 1967. *On Judaism*. Edited by Nahum N. Glatzer. New York, NY: Schocken Books.

　1969. "Of God Who Hides His Face." In *The Dimensions of Job: A Study and Selected Readings*. Edited by Nahum N. Glatzer, 56–64. Eugene, OR: Wipf and Stock Publishers.

Burrell, David B. 2008. *Deconstructing Theodicy: Why Job Has Nothing to Say to the Puzzle of Suffering*. Ada, MI: Brazos Press.

Buytendijk, F. J. J. 1961. *Pain*. Translated by Ade O'Shiel. London: Hutchinson of London.

Bibliography

Cavell, Stanley. 1976. *Must We Mean What We Say: A Book of Essays*. Cambridge: Cambridge University Press.

1979. *The Claim of Reason: Wittgenstein, Skepticism, Morality, and Tragedy*. Oxford: Oxford University Press.

1988. *In Quest of the Ordinary: Lines of Skepticism and Romanticism*. Chicago, IL: University of Chicago Press.

Cenkner, William, ed. 1997. *Evil and the Response of World Religion*. St. Paul, MI: Paragon House.

Dahl, Espen. 2014. *Cavell, Religion, and Continental Philosophy*. Bloomington, IN: Indiana University Press.

2015. "The Ambiguity of the Demonic in Tillich's View of Art." In *Transcendence and Sensoriness: Perceptions, Revelation and the Arts*. Edited by S. A. Christoffersen et al. Leiden: Brill.

2016. "Job and the Problem of Physical Pain." *Modern Theology* 32, no. 1: 45–83.

2017. "The Inner Tension of Pain and the Phenomenology of Evil." *International Journal of Philosophy and Theology* 78, no. 4–5: 396–406.

Dalferth, Ingolf. 2006a. *Leiden und Böses: Vom Schwierigen Umgang mit Widersinningem*. Leipzig: Evangelische Verlagsanstalt.

2006b. *Das Böse: Essay über die Denkform des Unbegreiflichen*. Tübingen: Mohr Siebeck.

Diamond, Cora. 1991. *The Realistic Spirit: Wittgenstein, Philosophy, and the Mind*. Cambridge, MA: MIT Press.

2008. "The Difficulty of Reality and the Difficulty of Philosophy." In *Philosophy & Animal Life*. Edited by S. Cavell, C. Diamond, et al. New York, NY: Colombia University Press.

Doak, Brian R. 2015. "Monster Violence in the Book of Job." *Religion and Violence* 3, no. 2: 269–278.

Bibliography

Douglas, Mary. 2002. *Purity and Danger: An Analysis of the Concepts of Pollution and Taboo*. London: Routledge.

Eagleton, Terry. 2010. *On Evil*. New Haven, CT: Yale University Press.

Girard, René. 1987. *Job: The Victim of His People*. Translated by Y. Freccero. Stanford, CA: Stanford University Press.

Glatzer, Nahum N., ed. 1969. *The Dimensions of Job: A Study and Selected Readings*. Eugene, OR: Wipf and Stock Publishers.

Hick, John. 2010. *Evil and the God of Love*. New York, NY: Palgrave Macmillan.

Hygen, Johan B. 1974. *Guds allmakt og det ondes problem*. Oslo: Universitetsforlaget.

van Inwagen, Peter. 2008. *The Problem of Evil*. Oxford: Oxford University Press.

Irenaeus. 2016. *Irenaeus: Against Heresies*. Translated by Phillip Schaff. Aeterna Press.

Jonas, Hans. 1987. "The Concept of God after Auschwitz: A Jewish Voice." *Journal of Religion* 67, no. 1: 1–13.

Jung, C. G. 2011. *Answer to Job*. Translated by R. F. C. Hull. Princeton, NJ: Princeton University Press.

Jüngel, Eberhard. 2003. *Wertlose Wahrheit*. Tübingen: Mohr Siebeck.

Kant, Immanuel. 1929. *Critique of Pure Reason*. Translated by Kemp Smith. London: Macmillan.

1960. *Religion within the Limits of Reason Alone*. Translated by T. S. Greene and H. H. Hudson. New York, NY: Harper Torchbooks.

2001. "On the Miscarriage of All Philosophical Trials in Theodicy." In *The Problem of Evil: A Reader*. Edited by Mark Larrimore, 224–234. Oxford: Blackwell.

Kermani, Navid. 2011. *The Terror of God: Attar, Job and the Metaphysical Revolt*. Translated by Wiwland Hoban. Cambridge: Polity Press.

Kierkegaard, Søren. 2009. *Repetition and Philosophical Crumbs*. Translated by M. G. Piety and E. F. Mooney. Oxford: Oxford University Press.

LaCocque, André. 1996. "Job and Religion at Its Best." *Biblical Interpretation* 4, no. 2: 131–153.

    2007. "The Deconstruction of Job's Fundamentalism." *Journal of Biblical Literature* 126, no. 1: 83–97.

Lactantius. 2001. "The Wrath of God." In *The Problem of Evil: A Reader*. Edited by Mark Larrimore, 46–52. Oxford: Blackwell.

Larrimore, Mark, ed. 2001. *The Problem of Evil: A Reader*. Oxford: Blackwell. 1990.

Leder, Drew. 1990. *The Absent Body*. Chicago, IL: Chicago University Press.

Leibniz, Gottfried Wilhelm. 2017. *Theodicy: Essays on the Goodness of God, the Freedom of Man, and the Origin of Evil*. Whithorn: Anodods Books.

Levenson, Jon D. 1988. *Creation and the Persistence of Evil: The Jewish Drama of Divine Omnipotence*. New York, NY: Harper and Row.

Levinas, Emmanuel. 1987. *Time and the Other*. Translated by R. Cohen. Pittsburgh, PA: Duquesne University Press.

    1998. "Transcendence and Evil." In *Job and the Excess of Evil*. Edited by Philippe Nemo. Translated by Michael Kigel, 165–182. Pittsburgh, PA: Duquesne University Press.

    2006. *Entre Nous*. Translated by Michael B. Smith and Barbara Harshav. London: Continuum.

Løgstrup, Knud Eilert. 1995. *Skabelse og Tilintetgørelse: Religionsfilosofiske Betragtninger. Metafysik IV*. Copenhagen: Gyldendal.

Luther, Martin. 2001. "Preface to the Book of Job." In *The Problem of Evil: A Reader*. Edited by Mark Larrimore, 135. Oxford: Blackwell.

Mackie, J. L. 1971. "Evil and Omnipotence." In *The Philosophy of Religion*. Edited by Basil Mitchell, 92–104. Oxford: Oxford University Press.

Bibliography

Maimonides. 2000. *The Guide of the Perplexed* (Part II, Ch. 23). In *The Jewish Philosophy Reader*. Edited by Daniel H. Frank, Oliver Leaman, and Charles H. Manekin, 73–78. Abingdon: Routledge.

Meister, Chad. 2012. *Evil: A Guide for the Perplexed*. London: Continuum.

Moltmann, Jürgen. 1974. *The Crucified God: The Cross of Christ As the Foundation and Criticism of Christian Theology*. Translated by R. A. Wilson and John Bowden. London: SCM Press.

   1981. *The Trinity and the Kingdom of God*. Translated by Margaret Kohl. London: SCM Press.

Morriston, Wesley. 1996. "God's Answer to Job." *Religious Studies* 32, no. 3: 339–356.

Nemo, Philippe. 1998. *Job and the Excess of Evil*. Translated by Michael Kigel. Pittsburgh, PA: Duquesne University Press.

Newsom, Carol A. 2009. *The Book of Job: A Contest of Moral Imagination*. Oxford: Oxford University Press.

Phillips, D. Z. 1993. *Wittgenstein and Religion*. London: Macmillan.

   2004. *The Problem of Evil and the Problem of God*. London: SCM Press.

Pihlström, Sami. 2013. *Pragmatic Pluralism and the Problem of God*. New York, NY: Fordham University Press.

Pihlström, Sami and Sari Kivistö. 2016. *Kantian Anti-Theodicy: Philosophical and Literary Varieties*. New York, NY: Palgrave Macmillan.

Plantinga, Alvin. 1971. "The Free Will Defense." In *The Philosophy of Religion*. Edited by Basil Mitchell, 105–120. Oxford: Oxford University Press.

Raz, Yosefa. 2014. "Reading Pain in the Book of Job." In *The Book of Job: Aesthetics, Ethics, Hermeneutics*. Edited by Leora Batnitzky and Ilana Pardes, 85–1004. Berlin: De Greuter.

Ricoeur, Paul. 1967. *The Symbolism of Evil*. Translated by Emerson Bachana. Boston, MA: Beacon Press.

2004. *The Conflict of Interpretations*. Translated by Don Ihde, Kathleen McLaughlin, et al. London: Continuum.

2007. *Evil: A Challenge to Philosophy and Theology*. Translated by John Bowden. London: Continuum.

Scarry, Elaine. 1985. *The Body in Pain: The Making and Unmaking of the World*. Oxford: Oxford University Press.

Seeskin, Kenneth. 2000. "Job and the Problem of Evil." In *The Jewish Philosophy Reader*. Edited by D. H. Frank, O. Leaman, and C. H. Manekin. New York, NY: Routledge.

Seow, C. L. 2013. *Job 1–21: Interpretation and Commentary*. Grand Rapids, MI: Eerdmans Publishing Company.

Sobrino, Jon. 1978. *Christology at the Crossroads*. Translated by J. Drury. New York, NY: Orbis Books.

Soelle, Dorothee. 1975. *Suffering*. Translated by E. R. Kalin. Philadelphia, PA: Fortress Press.

Stump, Eleonore. 2012. *Wandering in Darkness: Narrative and the Problem of Suffering*. Oxford: Oxford University Press.

Surin, Kenneth. 1983. "Theodicy?" *Harvard Theological Review* 76, no. 2: 225–247.

Swinburne, Richard. 1998. *Providence and the Problem of Evil*. Oxford: Clarendon Press.

Taylor, Charles. 2007. *A Secular Age*. Cambridge, MA: Belknap Press of Harvard University Press.

Tennessen, Herman. 1973. "A Masterpiece of Existential Blasphemy: The Book of Job." *The Human World* 13: 1–10.

Tillich, Paul. 1978. *Systematic Theology. Volume 1*. London: SCM Press.

1988. "Das Dämonische: Ein Beitrag zur Sinndeutung der Geschichte." In *Writings on Religion*. Edited by Robert P. Scharlemann. Berlin: De Gruyter.

Bibliography

Tilley, Terrence W. 2000. *Evils of Theodicy*. Eugene: Wipf and Stock Publishers.

Verbin, N. 2010. *Divinely Abused: A Philosophical Perspective on Job and His Kin*. London: Continuum.

Wiesel, Elie. 1976. *Messengers of God: Biblical Portraits and Legends*. Translated by Marion Wiesel. New York, NY: Touchstone.

  2006. *Night*. Translated by Marion Wiesel. London: Penguin.

Williams, Rowan. 2007. *Wrestling with Angels: Conversations in Modern Theology*. London: SCM Press.

  2016. *On Augustine*. London: Bloomsbury.

Wittgenstein, Ludwig. 2009. *Philosophical Investigations*. Translated by G. E. M. Anscombe, P. M. S. Hacker, and J. Schulte. Oxford: Wiley-Blackwell.

Wray, T. J. and Gregory Mobley. 2005. *The Birth of Satan: Tracing the Devil's Biblical Roots*. New York, NY: Palgrave Macmillan.

Cambridge Elements

Religion and Violence

James R. Lewis
University of Tromsø

James R. Lewis is Professor of Religious Studies at the University of Tromsø, Norway, and the author and editor of a number of volumes, including *The Cambridge Companion to Religion and Terrorism*.

Margo Kitts
Hawai'i Pacific University

Margo Kitts edits the *Journal of Religion and Violence* and is Professor and Coordinator of Religious Studies and East-West Classical Studies at Hawai'i Pacific University in Honolulu.

ABOUT THE SERIES

Violence motivated by religious beliefs has become all too common in the years since the 9/11 attacks. Not surprisingly, interest in the topic of religion and violence has grown substantially since then. This Elements series on Religion and Violence addresses this new, frontier topic in a series of ca. fifty individual Elements. Collectively, the volumes will examine a range of topics, including violence in major world religious traditions, theories of religion and violence, holy war, witch hunting, and human sacrifice, among others.

Cambridge Elements

Religion and Violence

Printed in the United States
By Bookmasters